LONG CIRC
WAL
IN THE
PEAK DISTRICT
- Vol. 2

by

JOHN N. MERRILL

Maps and photographs by John N. Merrill

TRAIL CREST PUBLICATIONS Ltd.,
- *"from footprint to finished book."*

1994

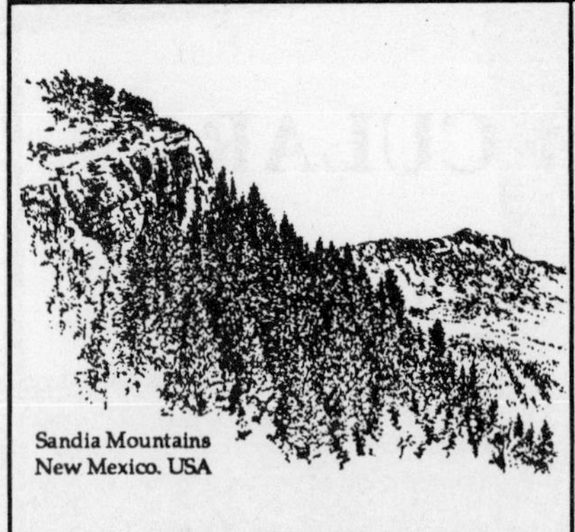

Sandia Mountains
New Mexico. USA

TRAIL CREST
PUBLICATIONS
Ltd.

Milne House
Speedwell Mill
Miller's Green
Wirksworth
Derbyshire
DE4 4BI

(01629) 826354
(01629) 826354

Edited, typeset, designed, paged, printed, marketed and distributed by John N Merrill.

First Published - March 1993.
Reprinted June 1993. This edition August 1994

ISBN 1 874754 09 8

Printed on 100% recycled paper.

U.S.A. office - P.O. Box 124, Santa Rosa, New Mexico 88435 U.S.A.

<u>**Please note**</u> - The maps in this guide are purely illustrative. You are encouraged to use the appropriate 1:25,000 O.S. map.

Meticulous research has been undertaken to ensure that this publication is highl accurate at the time of going to press. The publishers, however, cannot be hel responsible for alterations, errors or omissions, but they would welcome notifi cation of such for future editions.

Typeset in - Bookman - bold, italic and plain 9pt and 18pt.

Printed and designed by - Footprint Press Ltd./John N. Merrill at Milne House, Speedwell Mill, Miller's Green, Wirksworth, Derbyshire. DE4 4BL.

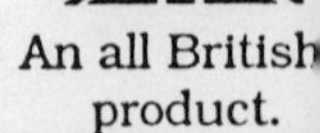

An all British product.

Cover sketch "Peak District Farm scene".
© Suncrest Ventures Ltd.,1994.

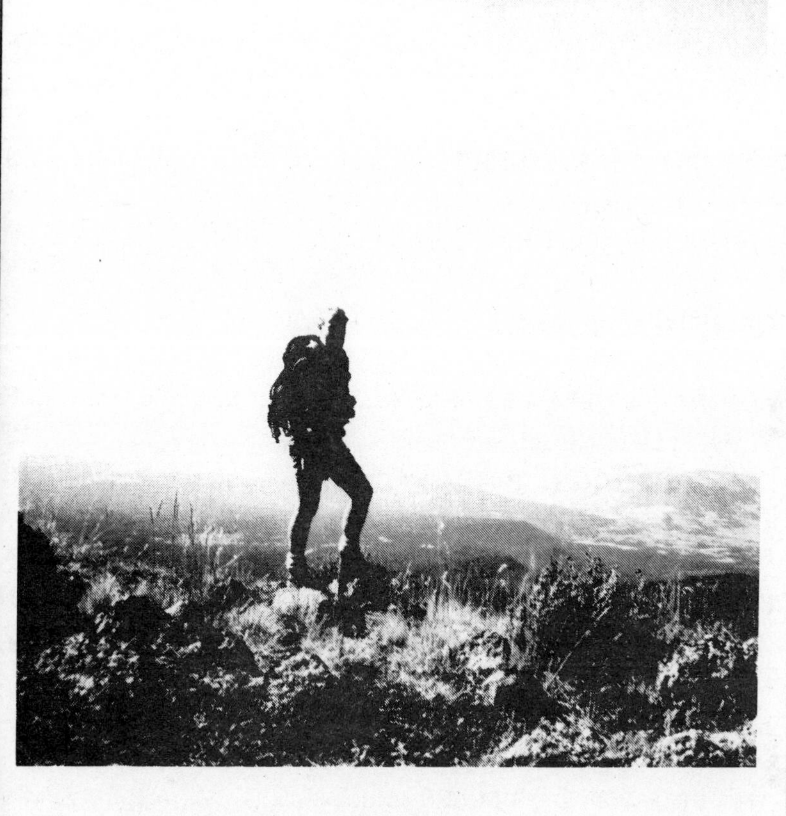

The author on the summit of Mt.Taylor (11,301ft.), New Mexico.

ABOUT JOHN N. MERRILL

Born in the flatlands of Bedfordshire he soon moved to Sheffield and discovered the joy of the countryside in the Peak District, where he lives. A keen walker who travels the world exploring mountains and trails. Over the last twenty years he has walked more than 150,000 miles and worn out over sixty pairs of boots. He has written more than 120 walk guides to areas in Britain and abroad, and created numerous challenge walks which have been used to raise more than £500,000 for charity. New Mexico, USA is his second home.

CONTENTS

Page No.

INTRODUCTION

There is only one way to appreciate and enjoy the countryside, and that is by walking. The flowers, the birds, work on the farms, historical features and scenic highlights are all encompassed in the walks in this book. Apart from the three at the end, all of the walks are between nine and twelve miles long— just the right length to enjoy the countryside and have time to look at the various features.

The book is divided into two halves, one dealing with walks in the gritstone countryside and the other with the limestone areas. All the routes are along rights of way, and I have personally walked them at least three times. They are circular, which means you can park your car in a village, walk in the area and return a different way to your starting point. The walking instructions and the rough map are designed to help you find your way round, and are intended to be complementary to the 1:25,000 Outdoor Leisure Maps - The White Peak, and The Dark Peak.

I do hope you enjoy these walks and that you will try them in the winter time as well as in the summer. Both seasons are colourful and have their own characteristics. If you find your way round and have gained pleasure from the walks, then my work has been worthwhile. Happy walking in this most beautiful slice of England.

John N. Merrill

The Peak District. 1993

The Saltcellar on Derwent Edge.

Monsal Dale.

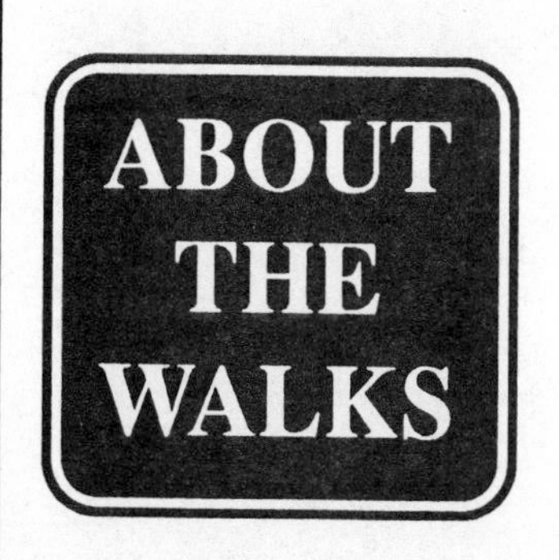

Whilst every care is taken detailing and describing the walk in this book, it should be borne in mind that the countryside changes by the seasons and the work of man. I have described the walk to the best of my ability, detailing what I have found on the walk in the way of stiles and signs. Obviously with the passage of time stiles become broken or replaced by a ladder stile or even a small gate. Signs too have a habit of being broken or pushed over. All the route follow rights of way and only on rare occasions will you have to overcome obstacles in its path, such as a barbed wire fence or electric fence. On rare occasions rights of way are rerouted and these ammendments are included in the next edition.

The seasons bring occasional problems whilst out walking which should also be borne in mind. In the height of summer paths become overgrown and you will have to fight your way through in a few places. In low lying areas the fields are often full of crops, and although the pathline goes straight across it may be more practical to walk round the field edge to get to the next stile or gate. In summer the ground is generally dry but in autumn and winter, especially because of our climate, the surface can be decidedly wet and slippery; sometimes even gluttonous mud!

These comments are part of countryside walking which help to make your walk more interesting or briefly frustrating. Standing in a farmyard up to your ankles in mud might not be funny at the time but upon reflection was one of the highlights of the walk!

The mileage for each walk is based on three calculations -

1. pedometer reading.
2. the route map measured on the map.
3. the time I took for the walk.

I believe the figure stated for each walk to be very accurate but we all walk differently and not always in a straight line! The time allowed for each walk is on the generous side and does not include pub stops etc. The figure is based on the fact that on average a person walks 2 1/2 miles an hours but less in hilly terrain.

ALPORT CASTLES - 12 MILES

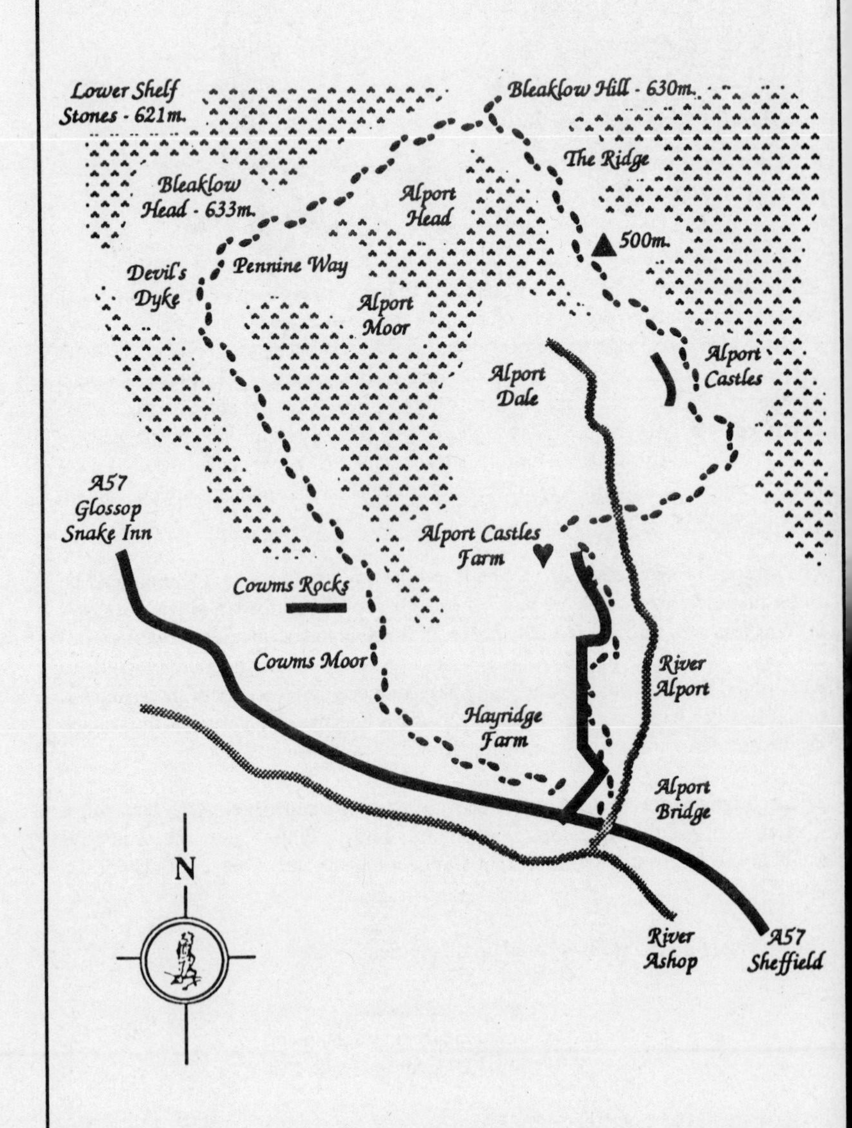

ALPORT CASTLES - 12 MILES

- allow 5 hours.

Alport Bridge—Alport Dale—Alport Castles—Bleaklow Hill — Devil's Dyke — Cowms Rocks — Alport Bridge.

O.S. MAP ***1:25,000 Outdoor Leisure Map - The Dark Peak.***

P ***- Limited roadside parking. Grid Ref. 142895***

- None on the walk; nearest Snake Inn.

Terrain: Peat and grass moorland. Only three miles of path; rest by compass bearing. Hard walking conditions—for experienced only.

ABOUT THE WALK - This is one of the hardest walks in the book. The distance is not great but the nature of the terrain saps one's energy, and as much of it has to be done by compass and is therefore, a walk for the more experienced. If you cannot use a compass don't attempt it, but by all means do the first two miles to see the historic farm and landslip. To the experienced person, this route should not present any problems.

WALKING INSTRUCTIONS - On the left-hand side of Alport Bridge ascend the stone stile and follow the footpath to the track from Hayridge Farm. On meeting this turn right and follow it for almost a mile to Alport Castles Farm. As you walk along, ahead on the right-hand side of the valley can be seen the huge landslip of Alport Castles. In the large barn of the farm on the first Sunday in July each year is held the Alport Castles Woodland Love Feast. The phrase "love feast" is a misnomer for it is a religious event of great antiquity. In ecclesiastical terms "love feast" means a "Feast of Charity," and here the rich feed the poor. The event originates from very early days, but its present form dates from the beginning of Methodism in the early half of the 18th century. There is a tradition that John Wesley preached at the barn. The service starts at 11 a.m. and the *"love feast"* at 1-30 p.m.—baskets of sliced cake are handed round followed by water.

On reaching the farm turn right and double back on your route slightly to gain the river Alport. Cross it via the footbridge and begin the steady half mile climb up the valley side to the top edge of the landslip, the largest in the Peak District. Standing on the edge you can appreciate its size and see where a huge piece of the valley slid downwards.

From the edge turn left and follow the footpath along the crest of the valley for a short distance. Where it turns right and descends towards Howden Reservoir, keep straight ahead. A compass is now necessary with the triangulation pillar, height 1,661 feet (500m), on the summit of Westend Moor being the first aim point. From here cross Alport Moor and ascend "The Ridge" to Alport Head and the summit of Bleaklow Hill. As you cross the grass and peat moorland, grouse let out their startled cry and fly sporadically away. In winter you will often see a mountain hare—principally a Scottish animal but several exist on this moorland. During the winter they are at their most conspicuous, as their coats change from brown to a white making identification easy.

From Bleaklow Hill bear left and follow the wooden stakes to Bleaklow Head. Here you join the Pennine Way and a distinct path leading down to the Snake Road. Use this for a little under a mile before bearing left and going by compass again. It is also worthwhile to maintain your high ground and go from Bleaklow Head to Higher Shelf Stones, a very good vantage point with Glossop and Longdendale in front. Just east of the summit, and needing a little bit of searching to find, are the remains of a plane which came down during the war. The engines, parts of the fuselage and wings are scattered over a wide area.

In the vicinity of Alport Low leave the footpath and begin the moorland crossing. First aim for the spot height, 1,759 feet (538m), on Over Wood Moss, and after this weave your way over the moors where the delicate cotton grass bends in the breeze. This two mile section is far harder than you think. As you walk along, on your left you have good views of Alport Castles and, with the sun in the west in the afternoon, this area is the best location for photographing the landslip. Near the end of the moorland bear right to Cowms Rocks. From these descend Cowms Moor to the access point of the "Open Countryside," using the footpath which runs along the course of a Roman Road. Once here the worst is over; simply turn left and follow the track past Hayridge Farm until you reach your starting-out path on your right. Turn right over the stile and descend through the trees back down to Alport Bridge, ending a moorland walk which increases your respect for Bleaklow.

Alport Castles Farm.

Ashopton Viaduct and Ladybower Reservoir - Derwent Edgewalk.

KINDER DOWNFALL - 8 MILES

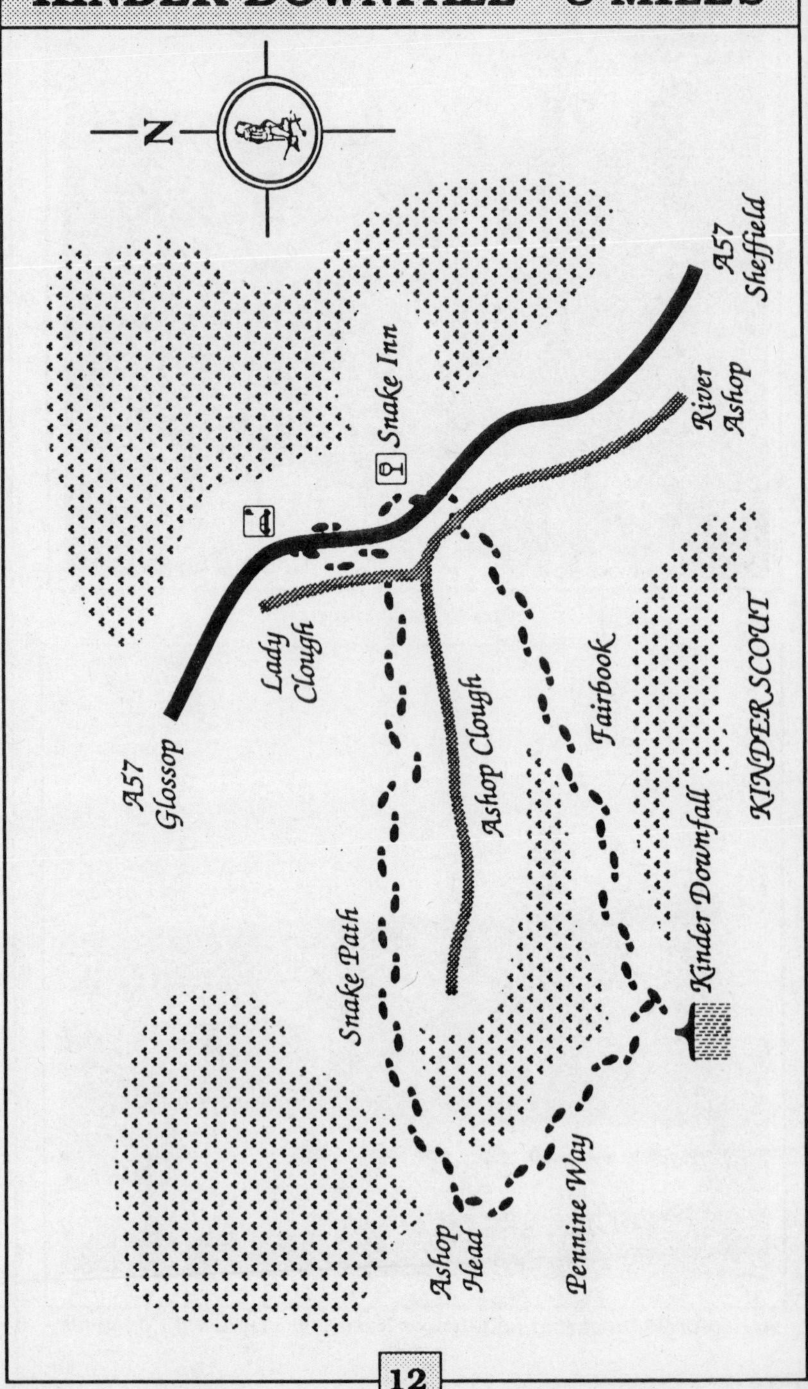

KINDER DOWNFALL - 8 MILES

- allow 3 hours.

The Snake Inn—Snake Path—Ashop Head—Pennine Way—Kinder Downfall— Fair Brook — Snake Inn.

O.S. MAP ***- 1:25,000 Outdoor Leisure Map - The Dark Peak.***

P ***- Birchen Clough. Grid Ref. 109914***

- Snake Inn

Terrain: Footpaths in the cloughs and along Pennine Way. Compass crossing from Downfall to Fair Brook.

ABOUT THE WALK - Kinder Downfall is one of the showpieces of the peak whose bleak surroundings are in the summer an alluring prospect. In the winter the fall reaches its zenith — coating the one hundred foot drop are sheaths of icicles which create a picture of sparkling beauty. This walk takes you to it, and your return over part of Kinder Scout brings you to another waterfall which likewise is best seen in winter.

WALKING INSTRUCTIONS - From the car park cross the road and gain the path down into Lady Clough. Bear left through the Snake Plantation to the main Snake Path. Bear right along it over the footbridge and follow the track close to the River Alsop and begin ascending to the "Open Country" and Ashop Clough. The path keeps to the right-hand side of the river and you ascend gradually for three miles. At the summit of the clough turn left and join the wide track which will take you all the way to the downfall. You are now walking along part of the Pennine Way.

The ascent is steep to start with, but having gained the rim of Kinder Scout the walking is easy along a wide track around its perimeter. Soon you see ahead the gritstone buttress that surrounds the downfall. In summer the word "downfall" is a misnomer for, if a wind is blowing, the water instead of falling down is blown back onto the plateau, meaning a soaking if you are not alert. The peat plateau is slippery walking in summer, but in winter the surface is frozen and walking is much easier. It is a good plan, if it is your first time up here, to come during the warmer months and get the lay of the land. Then, in the winter, return and see the area at its best. It is worth the effort to feel the cold wind flush your cheeks and be able to see the downfall in all its glory. It will be a day you won't forget. You could see some climbers ascending the ice-fall of the downfall—it is a pleasant and exposed climb and impressive to watch.

From the downfall the hard part of the walk begins. The surface of the plateau is covered with peat groughs, and in profile is like a saw's edge. To cross it involves ascending and descending most of these small hollows, although some you can jump across. You must take a compass bearing from the downfall to the head of Fair Brook — if you haven't a compass return the way you came, for even in summer it is folly to cross the unpathed mass without one. It is only a mile across but the nature of the terrain will make the crossing take about half an hour or more. It does have some consolations—as you walk through the peat and bilberries, grouse flutter away in your wake. They wait until you are almost on top of them before revealing their presence by an eerie, startled cry. In the winter, mountain hares will be seen, their white coats making them very conspicuous against the dark brown peat.

On reaching Fair Brook descend to the left and in due course a path will materialise above the brook further down. Another path exists on the high ground overlooking the clough, but personally I prefer the lower one. The descent from the plateau is steep at first, and there is a waterfall here which tumbles down a series of steps. In winter the fall is a frozen mass, posing a small problem to ice-climbers. The brook further down has created many pools with small and very picturesque waterfalls which after a warm day are very inviting. At the end of the clough turn left and cross the river Ashop via the wooden foot bridge. Ascend through the trees to the road (A57), and turn left and walk up it to the Snake Inn and onto the car park, ending a short but adventurous walk on Kinder.

Kinder Downfall.

DERWENT EDGE - 9 MILES

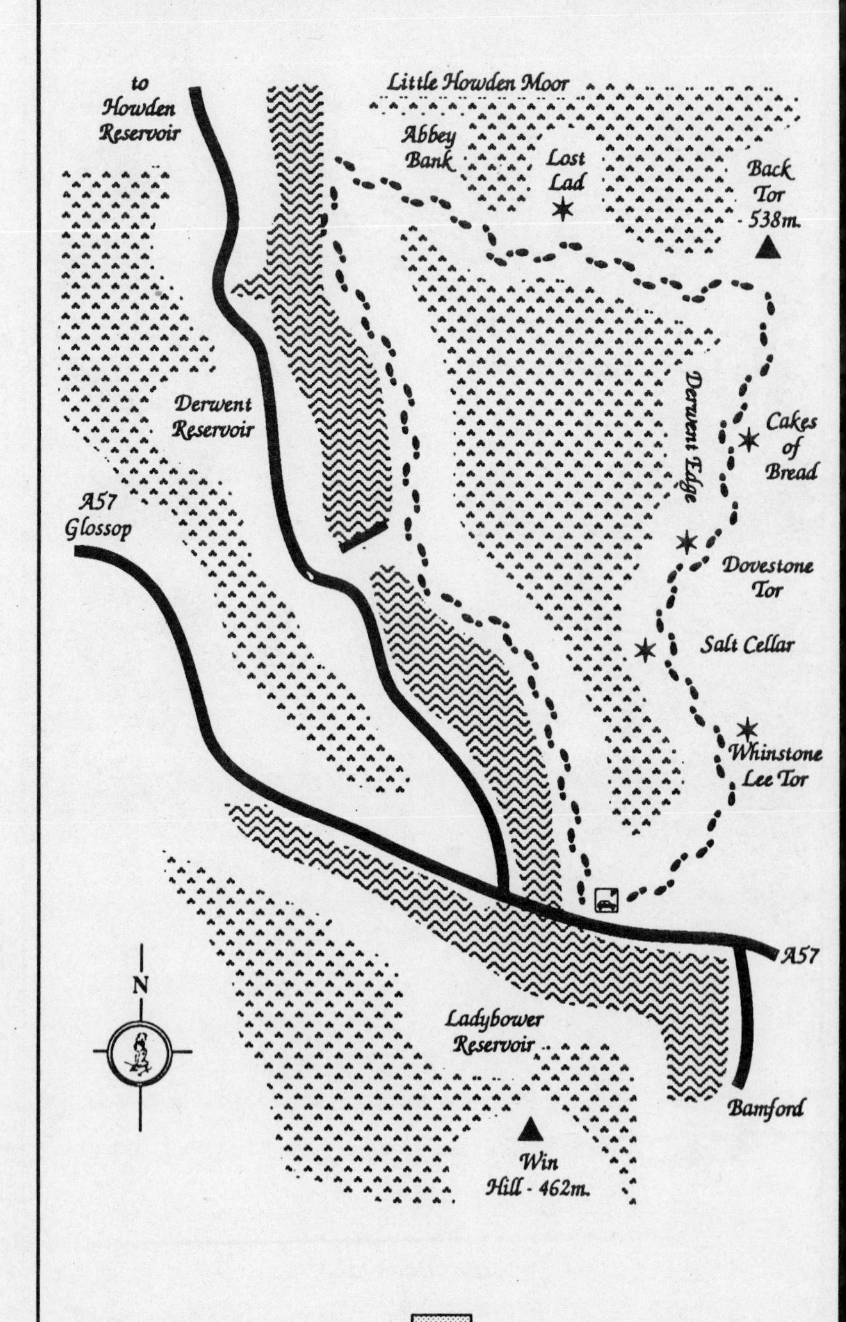

DERWENT EDGE - 9 MILES

- allow 3 1/2 hours

Ashopton viaduct — Ladybower Reservoir - Derwent Reservoir —Abbey Bank — Lost Lad— Derwent Edge—Ashopton viaduct.

- 1:25,000 Outdoor Leisure Map - The Dark Peak.

- Beside the A57, Gride Ref. 197864. Another on the A57 1/2 mile to the west at Grid Ref. 187865.

- None. Nearest - Ladybower Inn, 1/2 mile east on the A57.

Terrain: First half of walk, track walking. Second half along footpaths over grass moorland.

ABOUT THE WALK - Whatever the season this route will always delight the walker. The views, weird rock formations, the stretches of water and the woodland all combine to make it a memorable experience. For the first part of the walk you walk beside the reservoirs and pass the site of the now lost village of Derwent. You return along a gritstone edge whose vantage point is unsurpassed.

WALKING INSTRUCTIONS - Begin the walk from the lay-by just in front of Ashopton viaduct on the A57 road at Ladybower Reservoir, the last and largest of the three reservoirs to be constructed in Derwent Dale. Work began in 1935 and was completed ten years later; it covers a surface area of 504 acres and holds 6,300 million gallons of water. During construction Ashopton and Derwent had to be submerged.

From the viaduct follow the Water Board road along the right-hand side of the reservoir for the better part of four miles. After the first mile you come to Grain Foot Clough on your right with a small stream running down it. On your left and close to the reservoir's edge can be seen the walls, gateposts and outline of Grainfoot Farm, which was demolished when the reservoir was being constructed. A little over half a mile later you come to another clough with Mill Brook tumbling down it. This is the site of Derwent village.

Before the flooding of the valley all the houses were demolished, together with the church, but the spire was left standing and for two years until December 15th, 194 stood forlornly far out in the reservoir. It was a frequent challenge to swim out to it, while some are reputed to have climbed it. Not far from the church was located Derwent Hall, built by the Balguy family in 1672 and from 1932 used as a Youth Hostel until it was demolished. The gate posts were removed and now stand at the entrance to the reservoir wall. The 17th century packhorse bridge was likewise moved from the village and has been erected at Slippery Stones towards the head of the valley. Little can be seen of the village today, except for the walls of the vicarage, although during periods of dry weather when the reservoir's level drops it is often possible to locate mounds of stones denoting the former houses.

Continue along the now tarmacadamed road and where it dips down to the wall of Derwent Reservoir bear right along the rough track. In due course you walk beside this reservoir — the dam wall is 114 feet high and 1,110 feet long and at its base measures 178 feet. After approximately 1 1/2 miles the track begins to curve into a wide clough with the Abbey Brook running through it. Just as you begin to curve turn right along the footpath and ascend first through trees and then over grassy hillside to the summit of Abbey Bank

As you ascend, don't look round until you reach the top. Then the view down on to Derwent and Howden reservoirs and the moorland of Bleaklow beyond can only be described as stunning. Despite the number of times I have sat there and gazed at the scene, I never fail to marvel at its beauty. One of my favourite times here is on New Year's Day — you can sit in perfect solitude with a leg of chicken and a bottle of whisky!

From Abbey Bank follow the footpath across the grass moorland to the gritstone rocks of Back Tor, 1 1/2 miles away. The path reaches the ridge of Derwent Edge just to the right of the rocks, and it is well worth while to turn left and ascend to the summit, 1,765 feet (538m) high. The view stretches over the bleak moorlands and in the distance Stocksbridge and its industrial chimneys can be seen. Looking down the way you came, over on your right you can see a large pile of stones. This is the cairn marking the resting place of Abraham, known as the Lost Lad (see my book — ***"Legends of Derbyshire"***). Following a snowstorm this young boy set off from Derwent village to gather his mother's sheep together, but another storm blew up and he became lost. He crawled under a rock and scratched the words, "Lost Lad." His body was found three months later and ever since then shepherds have placed a stone there, thus creating the memorial we see today.

Descend gradually from the summit and follow the wide footpath along the ridge of Derwent Edge. The gritstone boulders have weathered over the centuries, creating unusual shapes which have given rise to them being individually named. The first ones you come to, from Back Tor, are Cakes of Bread—these circular rocks over on your left look exactly like mounds of dough. After crossing the rocks of Dovestone Tor you pass close to the Salt Cellar on your right. The erosion force of the wind has weathered this tall pillar of rocks into a twenty foot high salt pot. The view from this area down on to Ladybower Reservoir, and towards the Hope Valley, is impressive. Over half a mile later you walk past Wheel Stones on your left; these large clumps of rocks are very reminiscent of horizontal stacks of car tyres.

Approximately 1/4 mile from these rocks turn right and descend from the edge for a short distance before turning left and walking underneath the slopes of Whinstone Lee Tor. Keep to a wide grass track which soon runs along side a forest on the right before going through a forest gate and following the track through the trees. In due course you descend close to a farm. Turn right and once through the gate follow the tarmacadamed road past the houses and round a corner until you are back at the starting point.

The Wheel Stones - Derwent Edge.

THE PEAKLAND RIDGE - 9 MILES

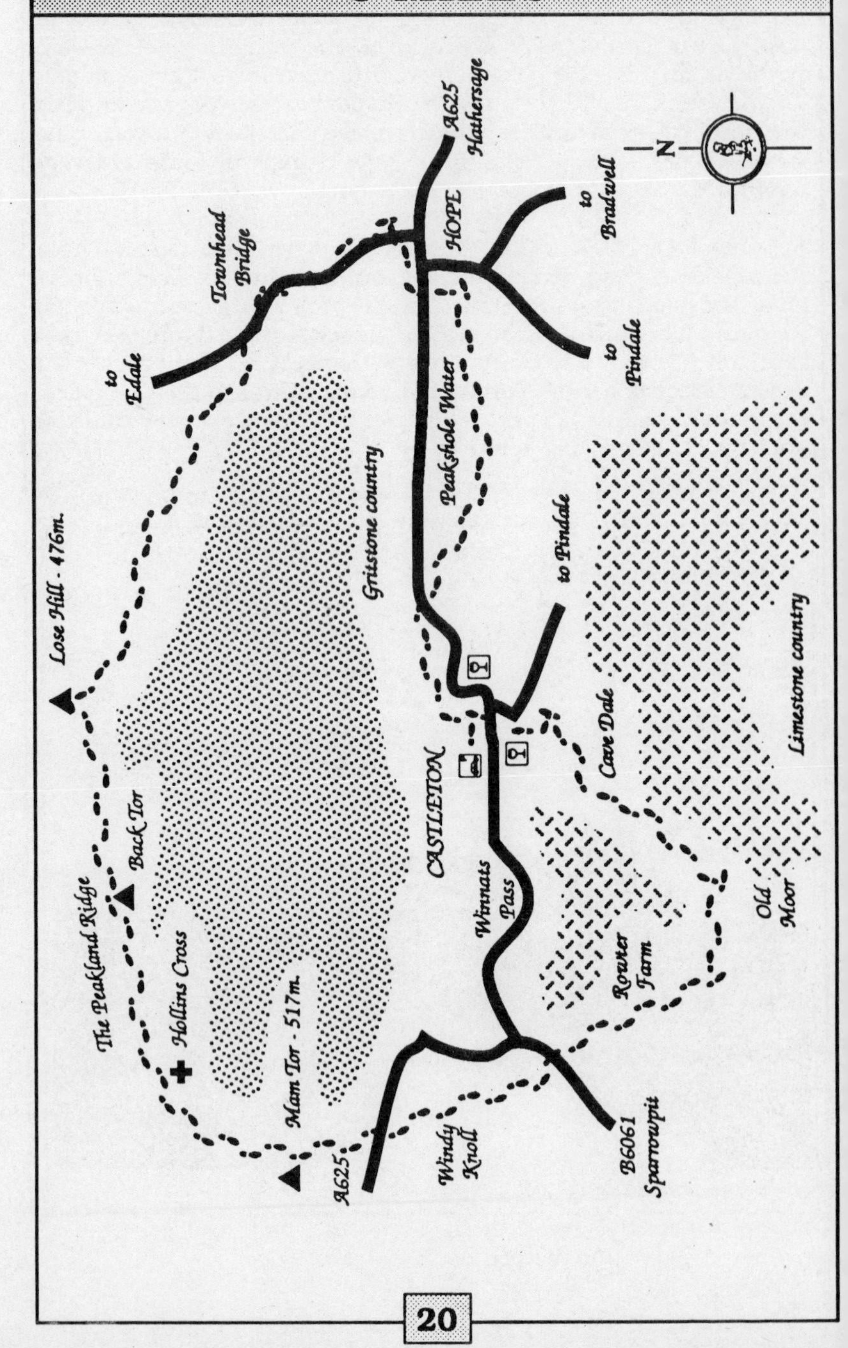

THE PEAKLAND RIDGE - 9 MILES

- allow 3 1/2 hours

Castleton—Peakshole Water—Hope—Lose Hill — Back Tor — Hollins Cross — Mam Tor — Windy Knoll — Old Moor — Cave Dale — Castleton.

1:25,000 Outdoor Leisure Map - The Dark Peak.

- Central Castleton.

Several in Castleton & Tea rooms. Old Hall Hotel, Cheshire Cheese Inn, Hope.

Terrain: Footpaths across fields and over the hills. About one mile of road walking.

ABOUT THE WALK - Between the summits of Lose Hill and Mam Tor is the finest ridge walk in Derbyshire, with distant views of the Hope and Edale valleys. Choose a clear day when the haze does not spoil the view and you will have a superlative walk!

WALKING INSTRUCTIONS - From Castleton go through the village on the Sheffield road, A625, heading towards Hope. As you near the out skirts of Castleton and the bridge over Peakshole Water turn right along a track signposted for Hope. You soon lose the track and begin following a path through the fields with the brook close by on your left. On meeting the road, south of Hope, turn left and walk beside the church into the village Near the main entrance to the church is the shaft of a Saxon cross, and inside the building are many interesting monuments. Two vertical grave slabs, on the right of the tower, are to two foresters of the Royal Forest of the Peak. The schoolmaster's chair bearing the date 1664 is near the pulpit and has a Latin motto carved on it which means, *"You cannot make a Scholar out of a block of wood."*

From the church cross the A625 and walk up the Edale road. Just before this crosses the river Noe (Townhead Bridge) turn left along the road to the C.H.A. guest house. Take the first track on your left and ascend towards Townhead Farm, but before entering the farmyard turn right along the sunken hedged lane. Now the ascent of Lose Hill begins in earnest, and soon you leave the hedges behind and climb the green hillside. Keep on the path to the summit — to take the path which runs under the summit to the base of Back Tor would be to admit defeat! Once on top you have a stunning panorama. Ahead is the Edale Valley with Edale village nestling at the foot of Grindsbrook Clough, while higher up the bleak moorland mass of Kinder stands out stark and awesome. Behind is Win Hill, Stanage and Bamford Edges and then the majestic sweep of the Hope Valley with Millstone Edge at the head.

Feeling as though you are walking in between two deep chasms, leave Lose Hill and go along the ridge to the rocky summit of Back Tor. Here you have a short but steep descent before continuing to Hollins Cross. The circular stone monument here was erected by members of the Long Eaton Rambling Club in memory of their founder member, John Hyett. The top has a metal plate which indicates the various footpaths radiating out from this point. Keep to the ridge and begin the gentle but long ascent to Mam Tor's summit.

As you climb you can see the single rampart ditch running around the summit plateau. This was an Iron Age fort and during recent excavations many Late Bronze Age items have been uncovered. Overlooking the Hope Valley is the loose face of Mam Tor which because of its geological formation has been nicknamed "Shivering Mountain." From the summit descend to the minor road to Edale, and here turn left to go down the field and across the main A625. Follow the grass track over the meadow of Windy Knoll to the Sparrowpit road, B6061. Cross this and walk up the road past Rowter Farm, from where the lane becomes a rough track as it goes over Old Moor. Turn left on meeting the next track and left again shortly afterwards, as sign posted, and begin to drop down towards Castleton. Part way along turn right and continue descending, but this time through the delightful limestone Cave Dale.

Ahead and above the limestone buttresses the dominant position of Peveril Castle can be appreciated. Further down the dale narrows and you squeeze past the limestone walls to emerge at Castleton Square, ending your walk. If you have time and energy left there are several places to visit in the village. The castle makes an attractive climb, for by sitting on the defence wall, you can gaze at the majestic line of the "Peakland Ridge" which you have walked along and can also peer down into Cave Dale. Castleton's church is also of considerable interest, possessing a Norman chancel arch and box pews.

Mam Tor from near Castleton, in winter.

Winnats Pass - Just off the route.

MOOR & VILLAGE - 12 MILES

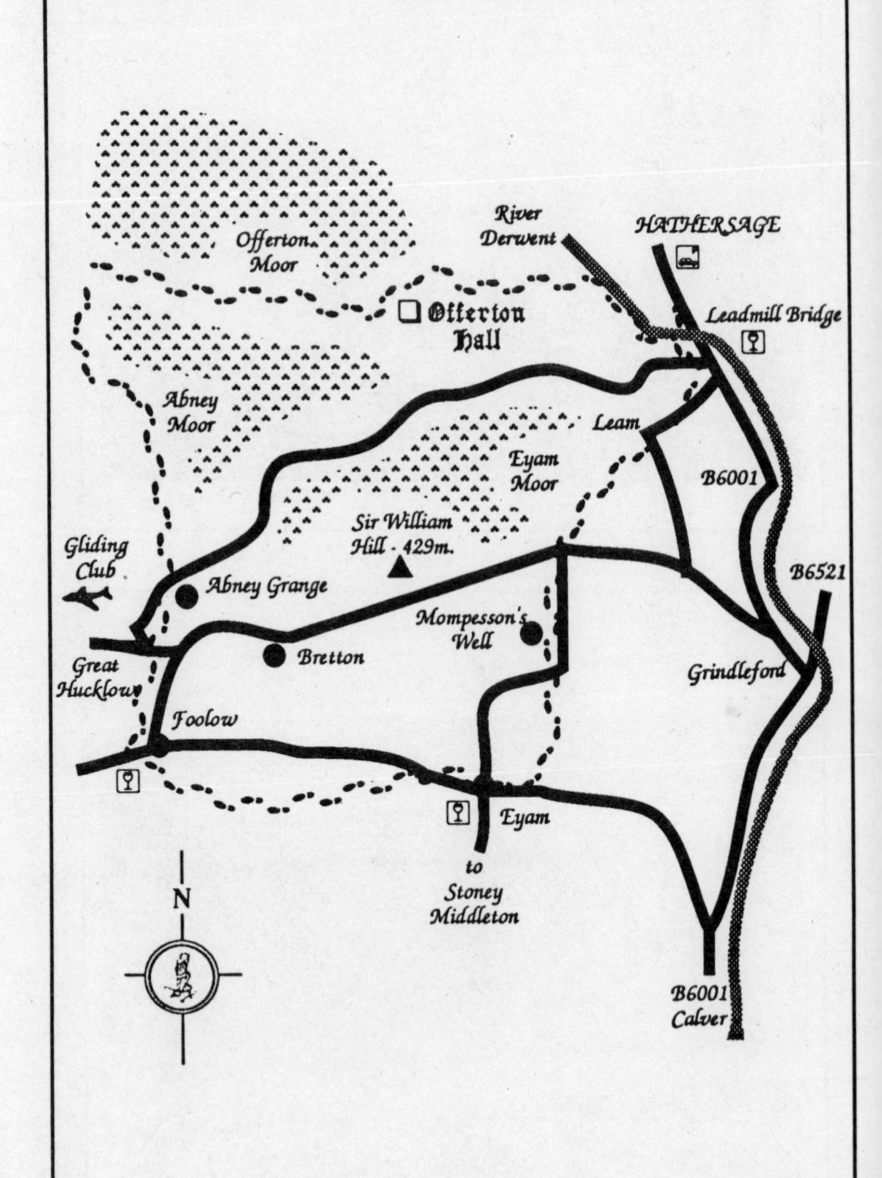

MOOR AND VILLAGE - 12 MILES

- allow 4 1/2 hours.

Hathersage — Leam — Eyam Moor - Mompesson's Well — Eyam — Foolow — Hucklow Edge — Abney Grange — Offerton Moor — Hathersage.

1:25,000 Pathfinder Series Sheet No. SK28/38 - Sheffield. 1:25,000 Outdoor Leisure Map - The White Peak - East sheet & The Dark Peak.

 ***- Central Hathersage.***

- Several in Hathersage and Eyam; and tea rooms. Plough Inn, Leadmill. Lazy Landlord, Foolow.

Terrain: Field and moorland walking along distinct paths. A little road walking at beginning. Two steep but short ascents at Hucklow Edge and Bretton Clough.

ABOUT THE WALK - Good viewpoints, fascinating villages and architecturally interesting houses are just three of the enjoyments of this walk. En route you pass by most of the key places associated with the plague in Eyam village. But it is the views you will remember most at the end — from Eyam Moor they are extensive but from the lip of Offerton Moor down on to the Hope Valley they are breathtaking.

WALKING INSTRUCTIONS - Leave Hathersage by the Grindleford road (B6001) and follow it for about 1/3 mile before taking the second road - shortly after The Plough Inn - on your right past Leam Farm. Beyond the farm you turn right through the stile and follow the wide path, at first close to the wall, before bearing right and crossing Eyam Moor. As you gradually ascend this heather-clad moorland you have an impressive view in front of Froggatt and Curbar Edges, while behind you Hathersage and Stanage Edge grow in splendour. Over to your right is a Bronze Age stone circle —you have to take a compass bearing to locate it, but the circle is clear with several small boulders around the edge; it is near Wet Witchens.

On reaching the "T" junction just east of Sir William Hill, keep straight ahead and follow the road towards Eyam village. A short distance down the road you see on your left the old ruins of New Engine Mine, where the boiler and engine house still remain. About 1860 a shaft was sunk here and reached a depth of 1,092 feet, making this the deepest lead mine in Derbyshire. It continued in operation until 1884. Shortly after the mine you pass a walled grass lane on your right, at the bottom of which is Mompesson's Well. In 1665 and 1666 the bubonic plague ravaged the villagers of Eyam and out of 350 people, 267 died from the plague. The guiding light of the village was the rector, William Mompesson, who helped the inhabitants to bear their plight with courage. Shortly after the plague started he drew an imaginary line around the village, sealing it off from the outside world. The well is one of the points of the boundary. Here Mompesson left money in vinegared water and a letter for the Earl of Devonshire stating the recent developments in the village. In return for the money, medical supplies were left.

Continue past the turning to Bretton on your right and where the road turns sharp right keep straight ahead. Descend the steep path and then the gentle lane into Eyam village, passing a well on your left which dates back to 1558. At the end of the lane is The Square and bull ring of Eyam — bull baiting was one of the attractions of the fairs in the 18th and 19th centuries. At the road turn right and walk up Church Street. Outside many of the houses you will see a small black plaque with white lettering, recording the persons who died in the house during the plague.

At the top of the street is the parish church of St. Lawrence. A visit to it is a must for there is so much of historical interest here attached to the plague. In the graveyard facing the road is a fine Celtic cross, and the grave to Katherine Mompesson, William Mompesson's wife, who died of the plague some twelve months after it had started. Inside the church is a pre-Norman font, Mompesson's chair and a beautiful inscribed book recording the dates and names of all the villagers who died during the plague. Close to the church are the Plague Cottages, where George Vicars the tailor received the plague-filled cloth and was the first to die from the disease a few days later. A little further along on your right is Eyam Hall, built by the Wright family in 1676, and opposite on the green are the village stocks.

Continue along the road and take the second lane on your left. Just after the "T" junction on your left, turn right along the hedged path in between the houses. This crosses numerous fields, the stone stiles keeping you on the correct route. In just over a mile you reach the road in front of Foolow village with its green, pond and cross. The cross is 14th century but the base is 19th century and was placed in this position in 1868. In front of it is a large boulder with a metal bull ring.

Turn right opposite the cross and walk along the Bretton road for just over 1/4 mile. Where it bears slightly right and climbs, go over the stile and cross the field. Bear a little to the left as you begin to ascend to the summit of Hucklow Edge. There are stone stiles all the way, but although this section is short it is surprisingly steep in its latter stages. At the top, simply cross the road and descend steeply to Bretton Brook before climbing once more to Abney Grange. This is rather a cruel route, but the scenery makes the effort worth it!

At Abney Grange turn left up the track to the road, but bear right just before crossing it and continue along the path over Abney Moor. As you walk along this grass covered moorland, the swish or the voices of people talking will be heard overhead as a glider from the nearby club soars past. You can see the club on your left and will no doubt witness a take-off. On reaching the wide track after a little over a mile, turn right and follow it. Ignore the turning down to Abney village and keep on the track, but half a mile later bear right and follow the path round the heathery Offerton Moor. On meeting the path from Abney turn left and go along it across the moor to the edge, over looking the Hope Valley. The view unfolds and is majestic in its proportions. The valley sweeps to your left and right the gritstone edges guard the skylines and houses and trees are scattered at random.

Descend to your right from the moor and at the lane turn left past Offerton Hall, part of which bears the date 1658. Just past it turn right through the gate and descend the grass track to the Derwent, where turn right and follow the path beside the river for a little over a mile. On reaching the road (B6001) turn left and retrace your route back into Hathersage village, ending a walk which one never tires of doing either in summer or winter.

Plague Cottage - Eyam.

EDGE & RIVER - 9 MILES

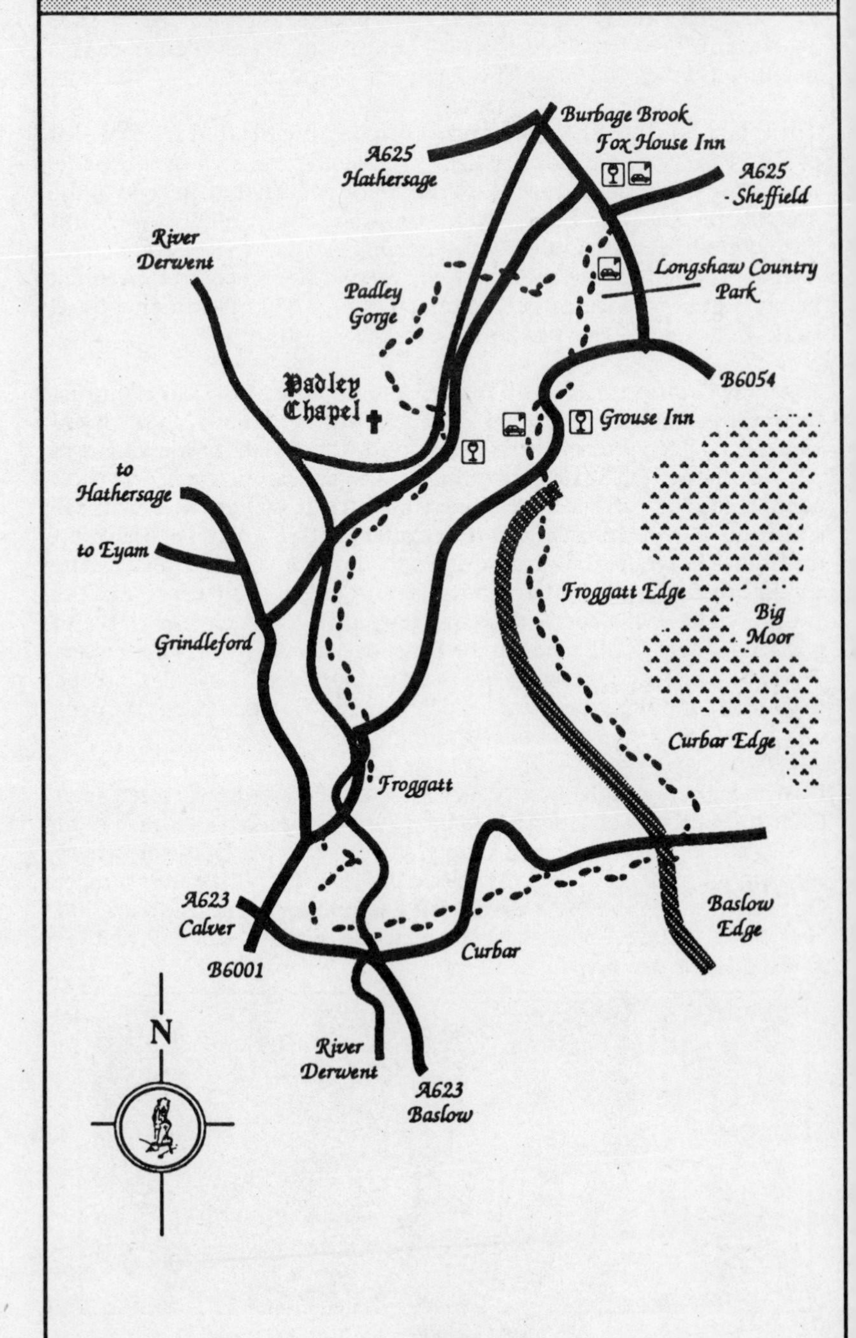

EDGE AND RIVER - 9 MILES

- allow 3 1/4 hours.

Fox House — Froggatt Edge — Curbar Edge— Curbar — Froggatt — Grindleford — Padley Gorge —Fox House.

1:25,000 Outdoor leisure map - The White Peak - East Sheet. 1:25,000 Pathfinder Series Sheet No. SK 28/38 - Sheffield.

- Near Fox House Inn.

- Fox House Inn. Maynard Arms, Grindleford. Cafe at Grindleford Station. Grouse Inn, near Froggatt Edge.

Terrain: Footpath walking along gritstone edges and beside river Derwent.

ABOUT THE WALK - The gritstone Edges are one of the natural wonders of the Peak District. This walk takes you along the top of two of the more impressive ones, from whose lip you have an extensive view over the central portion of the region Linking the walk together is the swift flowing Derwent river.

WALKING INSTRUCTIONS - Cross the road opposite Fox House Inn and enter the Longshaw Estate via the stone stile. Turn left along the road to the lodge, where turn right as signposted and descend the steps to follow the path around the building. It was formerly a shooting lodge for the Dukes of Rutland and dates from the early part of the 19th century. The drive ways through the estate were made by the "Bachelor Duke." Almost opposite the chapel go through the two gates and continue along the wide grass driveway through the Sheffield Plantation to the road (B6054), a little over a mile away. The plantation takes its name from the Sheffield Planting Company, which was founded in 1823 and owned this 100 acre wood comprising oak, silver birch and fir trees.

On reaching the road turn right and walk past the Grouse Inn and turn right on the path towards the car park. Turn left and follow the path across the stream and upto the B6054. Cross over and follow the wide track along the top of Froggatt and Curbar Edges. The walk along here until you reach the road for Curbar village is one of the most pleasant stretches to be found anywhere As you weave your way across the heather-clad top, the view to your right is impressive. Stoney Middleton with its surrounding bastions of limestone can be seen, while above is Longstone Moor and further right the prominent mast on Sir William Hill forms an important landmark. Directly below is the river Derwent which you can trace meandering past Froggatt and Grindleford villages.

Often the path follows the crest of the edge and you will be able to see those able-bodied climbers ascending the cracks and ledges which litter the vertical or overhanging rock. With barely no warning you leave Froggatt Edge and walk beside Curbar Edge — the "Cloggy of the Peak." It has some of the highest gritstone faces in the Peak District and the routes up them are both hard and sustained. One, because of the shape of a cleft, is perfectly named "Peapod." On reaching the minor road, turn right and begin heading down it towards Curbar. After a short distance you will see a footpath sign on your left; leave the road and descend the path to the outskirts of the village, thus cutting off the large corner on your right. Continue descending through the village, whose houses with their colourful gardens are always a joy to behold. At the bottom turn right and cross the old bridge over the Derwent before turning right and following the lane past Calver Mill. By a group of buildings this becomes a footpath running close to the river.

You walk past "The Goit," a special water channel made to take water to Calver Mill in order to operate its large water wheels. Scrapped during the last war, these were 24 feet in diameter and 17 feet wide On meeting the road from Froggatt, cross it and continue walking beside the river along its left-hand bank. Both coots and moorhen can be seen here and very often mallard ducks. Of the smaller birds, the charming pied wagtail flits across the water or wags its tail on a nearby rock.

Having past a fir wood on your immediate right, you gain the Froggatt road on the left-hand side of the bridge. Cross this, turn left and walk through Froggatt. Is there a village more beautiful than this one in the area? I doubt it. By keeping straight ahead you pass the cottages with their gardens full of radiant flowers and gain a walled track which later becomes a footpath as you cross meadow and woodland to the outskirts of Grindleford village. This is delightful walking and maintains the high quality you have enjoyed through the earlier part of the route.

You reach Grindleford almost opposite the garage on the left-hand side of the bridge. Turn right and walk beside the road, B6521, passing the Maynard Arms on your right and then turning left to descend the road to the station. Cross the railway bridge and follow the rough track to your left as it curves past Padley Mill. The bridge is just in front of Totley tunnel, completed in 1894 and the second longest in Britain at 3 miles and 950 yards. After the houses, turn right and ascend the rough track into Padley Gorge. If you have time available it is well worth while to carry on up the track before turning right and visit Padley Chapel; all that remains of a manor house built by the Padley family in the 14th century. Here in 1588 two Roman Catholic priests Robert Ludlam and Nicholas Garlick, were arrested on 12th July. They were hung, drawn and quartered in Derby twelve days later.

In Padley Gorge you can see the Burbage Brook tumbling its way through the maze of gritstone boulders. As you walk along look out for that small bird, the wren. There are several in this area and in the early morning their song is one of the prettiest to be heard. Emerging from the oak trees at the top of the gorge, continue a little further before turning right, crossing the wooden footbridge and ascending to the road, B6521. Cross this to the wooden stile and enter the Longshaw Estate - a couple of minutes later you are at the lake. The date of its construction is unknown, but it is assumed that it was made at the same time as the lodge in 1830. Follow the path around it to your right and begin ascending to the lodge through the "Rhododendron Walk." Naturally, the best time to go through here is in June when the bushes are a riot of colours and their fragrance fills the air.

Leaving the bushes behind you, continue walking along a grass track and past a line of beech trees to reach the gates beside the chapel and your outward route. From the trees you have a clear view of the Burbage valley with the gritstone edge on your right and the Iron Age fort, Carl Wark, on your left. Behind that is Higger Tor with its tall leaning block just discernible; it is 45 feet high and over hangs 15 feet from its base. At the gates turn left and retrace your steps back to Fox House, ending a walk which I am sure you will enjoy doing many times.

Curbar Edge.

CHATSWORTH PARK - 9 MILES

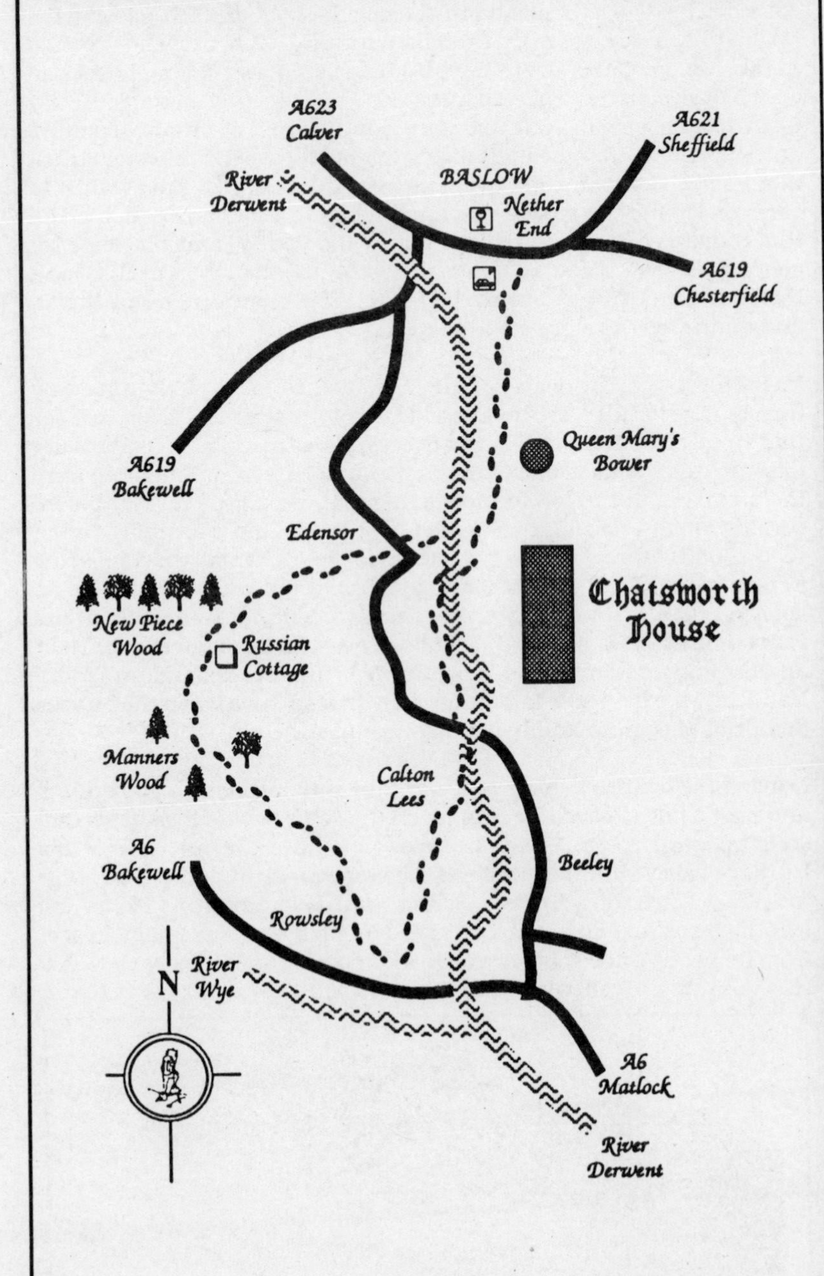

CHATSWORTH PARK - 9 MILES

- allow 3 1/2 hours

Baslow — Chatsworth Park — Calton Lees - Rowsley — Manners Wood — Calton Pastures — New Piece Wood — Edensor — Queen Mary's Bower — Baslow.

1:25,000 Outdoor Leisure map - The White Peak - East Sheet.

- Baslow (Nether End).

- Several in Baslow. Tearoom in Edensor.

Terrain: Footpaths across meadows and parkland. Track and path through woodland.

ABOUT THE WALK - This is the walk for lovers of serene beauty. First you traverse Chatsworth Park and then meander through pleasant woodland overlooking the "capital" of the Peak District, Bakewell. You then cross meadows and a wood. and once more your eyes gaze at Chatsworth, before visiting Edensor and regaining the village of Baslow.

WALKING INSTRUCTIONS - From the car park in Baslow, turn right and cross the bridge over Bar Brook in front of the delightful thatched cottage. Turn right again and follow the track to the large metal kissing gate, the entrance to Chatsworth Park. Continue along the track through the oak trees and then a path until you reach Queen Mary's Bower on your left — on the way you will more than likely see a grey squirrel. Once in the park the marvellous setting soon becomes apparent the fine lines of the house, the robust trees and the gentle curving meadows making the walk a constant pleasure.

Queen Mary's Bower and the shooting lodge high on your left are the two sole survivors of the Elizabethan Chatsworth House, built by Bess of Hardwick and her second husband, Sir William Cavendish, in 1557. Sir William died before much of the work had been done and the redoubtable Bess continued with it. When completed it had cost

£80,000. The fourth Earl of Devonshire began work in 1685 on the south front and became so involved and enjoyed rebuilding so much that he went on to redesign much of the house. Over the next two hundred years subsequent Dukes continued with the buildings and gardens to create today's scene.

Bess and her husband, George Talbot, the sixth Earl of Shrewsbury, were the guardians of Mary, Queen of Scots. The bower is named after her, and during her "imprisonments" at Chatsworth in the 1570s and '80s she often sat in the garden on top. From the bower you turn right and cross the three-arched bridge designed by James Paine in 1761. The mill formerly located near here was removed at this time and rebuilt nearer Beeley. Once over the bridge, turn left, cross the meadow and head for the group of beech trees above the river Derwent. From these either continue across the meadow or walk beside the river to the ruined mill. Here turn right to the road, cross it and follow the minor road into Calton Lees.

Keep left through the hamlet and just after the last house, where the road bears right, ascend the stone stile on your left and follow the signposted path to Rowsley, two miles away. Keep close to the gritstone wall to near its far corner where you ascend a ladder stile. Descend through the fields, heading southwards and through five gates. The fifth one brings you beside the river Derwent. As you descend, Beeley and Beeley Moor are on your left and Lindup Wood covers the slopes on your right. After the fifth gate cross the field to a ladder stile over a wooden gate on your right. Follow the path ahead to a wooden stile on the left-hand side of a gate before following the farm track through the fields and often close to the river to the houses of Rowsley. You emerge at Church Lane after walking under a railway bridge.

Turn right and ascend Church Lane, passing St. Katherine's church on your right. Continue ascending after the houses, now following a wide track through woodland. On meeting two green-painted metal bar gates take the left hand track. At the next meeting of tracks, again take the left-hand one. Shortly afterwards at the next junction, with Coombs Lane and Bakewell in the distance, turn right and ascend the track close to the edge on Manners Wood. At the top, on meeting a horizontal track turn left and 100 yards later turn right up another track to a stone wall. Follow the wall for a short distance to a clearing in the trees beside a pair of gateposts. The view from here down onto Bakewell is exceptional. Cross the stile here. and follow the path running diagonally leftwards through the young plantation. On reaching open country at a gate, turn right and follow the path beside the wood. A hundred yards later cross a wooden stile and your goal, New Piece Wood, can be seen ahead.

Descend through the field to your left, passing two gritstone water troughs on your right, before gaining a track which passes between two small plantations - Calton Plantations. Just through the gate turn right beside the wall and follow the path to Calton Houses. At the gate there turn left and follow the track overlooking Russian Cottage and into New Piece Wood. Once out of the trees and through the deer gate, the breathtaking view unveils itself. There in all its glory stands Chatsworth House, all the more splendid in the late afternoon when the setting sun enriches the golden building.

From the gate keep straight ahead, using the spire of Edensor church as your guide, and cross the pastureland. In this area you will more than likely see some of the herd of fallow deer which roam the park. You go in between two small circular clumps of trees before gaining the gate and steps down to the road on the left-hand side of the church. Turn right and walk through Edensor village, moved to its present site in 1837. The sixth duke, the "Bachelor Duke," did not want anything obstructing his view and so most of the houses were dismantled and rebuilt.

Edensor church, built by Sir Gilbert Scott in 1867, is well worth a visit. At the top of the graveyard can be seen many of the graves of the Dukes of Devonshire and the stone plaque recording President Kennedy's visit in 1963 to the grave of his sister Kathleen. Cross the road and follow the path which curves right through the beech trees before bearing left to the three-arched bridge. Here you turn left and retrace your steps back to Baslow. The area is so superb that this short duplication of route does not mar one's enjoyment of the final stages of this walk.

Edensor.

THE RIVER WYE - 9 MILES

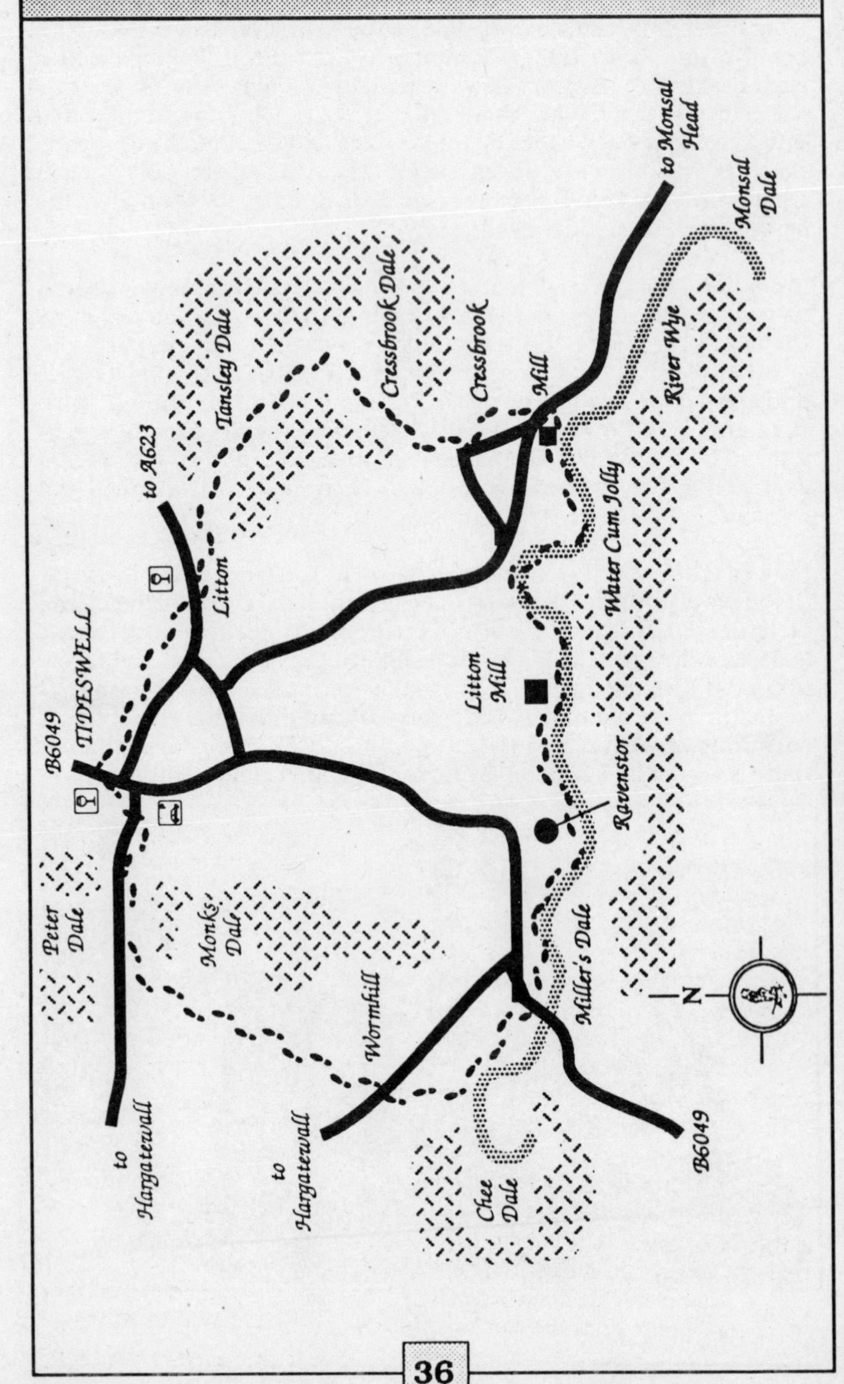

THE RIVER WYE - 9 MILES

- allow 3 1/2 hours.

Tideswell—Litton—Tansley Dale—Cressbrook Dale—Water Cum Jolly—Millersdale—Chee Dale—Wormhill—Monksdale House—Tideswell.

O.S. MAP ***- 1:25,000 Outdoor Leisure Map - The White Peak - East & West sheet.***

P ***- Cherry Square, Tideswell.***

- Several in Tideswell. Red Lion Inn, Litton. Angler's Rest, Millers Dale.

Terrain: Walking through limestone dales. A mile of road walking at beginning and end.

ABOUT THE WALK - Starting from one of the most interesting villages in Derbyshire, you weave your way through limestone dales with the ever majestic river Wye flowing beside you. The villages have interesting churches and halls, and you see some of the tallest limestone buttresses to be found in the Peak District.

WALKING INSTRUCTIONS - Leave Tideswell via the road to Litton and at the top of the first bend savour the excellent view of Tideswell church. This 14th century building, the most perfect in the country, can be fully appreciated from here, but leave its exploration to the end as a reward for completing the walk. A mile later in the centre of Litton village, take the Cressbrook road. At the first right-hand corner a walled lane comes in from your left; walk along this for a short distance before turning right and following the path down into Tansley Dale. This is delightful walking and half a mile later you are in Cressbrook Dale. It is rather cruel not to be able to walk down the valley, but you have to ascend the lefthand side before dropping down to the dale floor again. However, this does have the advantage that you have a marvellous view point from the top looking both up and down the valley.

Once down in the bottom again, both blackthorn and wood anemone are to be seen in flower in the spring. Cross the wooden footbridge and once more ascend, this time alongside the wood on your right to reach the road close to Cressbrook village. Over on your left on the other side of the valley can be seen Ravensdale, the limestone rock rising a hundred feet high and the face containing many rewarding rock climbs. On reaching the road bear left and descend to Cressbrook Mill on your right, once the work place of the poetical carpenter William Newton, nicknamed the *"Minstrel of the Peak."*

At the mill gates turn right and walk through the mill to the river Wye. Go to the right and follow the footpath alongside the river all the way to Litton Mill—this particular stretch is enchanting in the autumn when the trees exhibit their golden colours. In the summer both moorhen and coots can be seen on the wide expanses of water. Walk through Litton Mill to the road and continue along it all the way to Millersdale village. After half a mile you pass one of the natural wonders of Derbyshire in Ravens Tor a huge limestone buttress which overhangs 200 feet and has several alarming rock climbing routes up it. On meeting B6049 in the village, continue straight ahead. Where the Wormhill road comes into it on your right, turn right and twenty yards later on your left is the stile and footpath through Chee Dale. The path hugs the river Wye for most of the way and after about a mile curves round to your left to Chee Tor. Here you turn right and ascend the shallow dale to Wormhill, following a walled lane as you near the top.

On reaching the village road, Bagshawe Hall can be seen ahead. The Bagshawe family have been associated with Wormhill for centuries and are remembered for William Bagshawe who became known as the *"Apostle of the Peak"* in the 17th century. Walk up through the village and turn right down to the church which is well worth a visit. Its spire catches the eye immediately for it is not the type you expect to see in Derbyshire and is a copy of the Saxon spire at Stomping in Sussex.

Continue up the lane and where it divides at the vicarage take the left fork. Almost immediately on your left is a walled path. Follow this and cross the field, heading for a solitary hawthorn tree which has on its right a wooden stile. Keep straight ahead on a walled path, passing a track on your left and then descending to the road in between Monks and Peter Dale. In the final stages you leave the walled path behind and go through the field. At the road turn right and in just over a mile reach Tideswell—the house on the corner of the first road in the village has an exact replica of the church in the garden. Here turn left, walk along Sherwood Road and a few yards later turn right down Parke Road to reach the centre of Tideswell.

Having walked in the village's neighbourhood, a look at the church is a must. In the top left-hand corner of the graveyard can be seen William Newton's gravestone, in scribed *"Minstrel of the Peak."* The church interior with its carvings, stained-glass windows and brasses is well worth the half hour to see its many treasures before you return home.

Ravem's Tor, Millersdale.

MONSAL DALE - 9 MILES

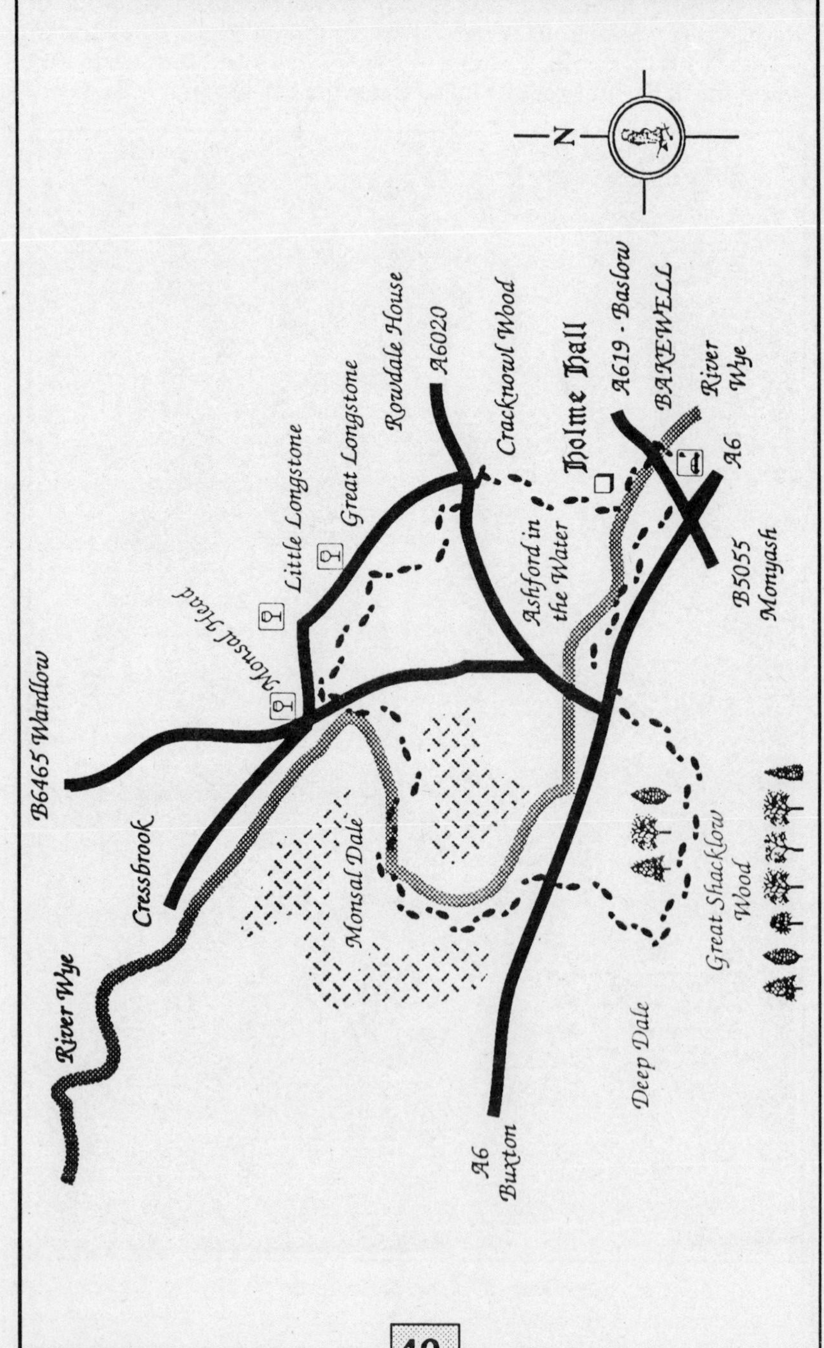

MONSAL DALE - 9 MILES

- allow 3 1/2 hours

Bakewell—Holme Hall—Rowdale House—Great Longstone—Little Longstone—Monsal Dale—Great Shacklow Wood—Ashford-in-the-Water—Bakewell.

1:25,000 Outdoor Leisure Map - The White Peak - East sheet.

- Central Bakewell.

Numerous in Bakewell. Monsal Head Hotel. Packhorse Inn, Little Longstone. Also - Great Longstone and Ashford in the Water.

Terrain: Footpaths across fields and through dales and woodland. Approximately 1 1/2 miles of road walking.

ABOUT THE WALK - Starting from the Peakland capital of Bakewell, this walk takes you into some of the finest and most interesting countryside of the National Park. It combines hill and dale, and en route you pass several historical features and an area rich in both birds and wild flowers.

WALKING INSTRUCTIONS - From Bakewell cross the magnificent 13th century five arched bridge over the Wye, before turning left and following the footpath beside the river to reach the road close to Holme Hall. Here go to the left and walk past the walled garden, and then turn right up the track on the left of this Jacobean hall with mullioned windows which was built in 1626. At the top of the track go through the wooden gate and continue ascending gradually through the field. At the far end you come to a walled track, where turn half left and cross the field. The path is not obvious but once part way round the field you will notice the stone stile. Once over this head for a solitary building 1/4 mile away, with a wood on its left.

From the right-hand side of the building bear slightly left and in due course reach a stile on the perimeter of Cracknowl Wood. Go over this and descend diagonally on a distinct path through the wood, before crossing a field and reaching the A6020 and Rowdale House. Turn left at the road and follow it to the first junction on your right, and then go under the railway bridge (Monsal Trail) and over the stone stile on your left. Shortly afterwards ascend another stile on your right and cross the fields to Great Longstone where the church with its rookery is well worth a visit. Much of the building is 13th century and the nave roof is 15th century with moulded beams.

Walk through the village along the road heading towards Little Longstone, passing the 18th century red-brick Longstone Hall on your right In Little Longstone notice the two stone uprights of the village stocks before reaching that wonderful view down on to Monsal Dale from Monsal Head. However many times one stands and looks at it, one never fails to be struck by its beauty. To your right the river Wye meanders down past Cressbrook Mill before gracefully curving round to enter Monsal Dale and sweeping past the flanks of Fin Cop. Crowning the scene is the five-arched railway viaduct, declared of historical and architectural interest.

Descend from Monsal Head by the path on the righthand side of the houses and walk down through the trees to cross the Wye via the footbridge just past the weir. The river supports a variety of birds, both coot and moorhen nesting in the reeds near the weir. During the summer the common sandpiper, marsh tits, redstarts bullfinches and several of the warbler family are usually seen. Continue walking down the dale and cross the A6 to the car park. The stile on your left indicates the footpath over into the bottom of Deep Dale. Once in the valley, ascend the wooden stile and instead of walking up the dale keep straight ahead and begin the gradual climb to Great Shacklow Wood. The footpath is signposted part way up. As you are ascending notice the various flowers: on the rocks you can see the yellow wall pepper and in spring the grass is full of wild primula and cowslips.

At the edge of the trees turn left as signposted and walk through Great Shacklow Wood, following a path on which many interesting items are to be seen. In due course it brings you close to the Wye where on your left is a great torrent of water flowing into the river. This is the mile-long water sough from Magpie Mine, near Sheldon, on which work started in 1873 and took eight years to complete at a cost of £18,000). A little further along the track you reach the ruins of a water mill on your left. The two large wheels are still in place and it is a great tragedy to see such an item of interest left in a state of decay. Originally the buildings crushed bones sent from London so that they could be used as manure.

The track keeps close to the river for another half mile before you reach the minor road from Sheldon. Turn left and at the A6 turn right and walk beside it until you can cross and enter Ashford-in-the-Water via the 17th century sheepwash bridge. You can see the sheep fold incorporated into the bridge on the right-hand side. The village was originally known as Ashford, but as there were others so named the suffix, *"in-the-water"* was added. The church dates from the 11th century but most of the current build ing is 14th century. As you enter by the main doorway you pass underneath a Norman tympanum, one of the handful to be seen in Derbyshire. Walk through the village and rejoin the A6. Turn left and almost immediately afterwards left again through a kissing gate to follow the footpath across the meadows to Bakewell. On the town's outskirts walk in between the houses before following the A6 into the centre, ending a walk of great interest and scenic beauty.

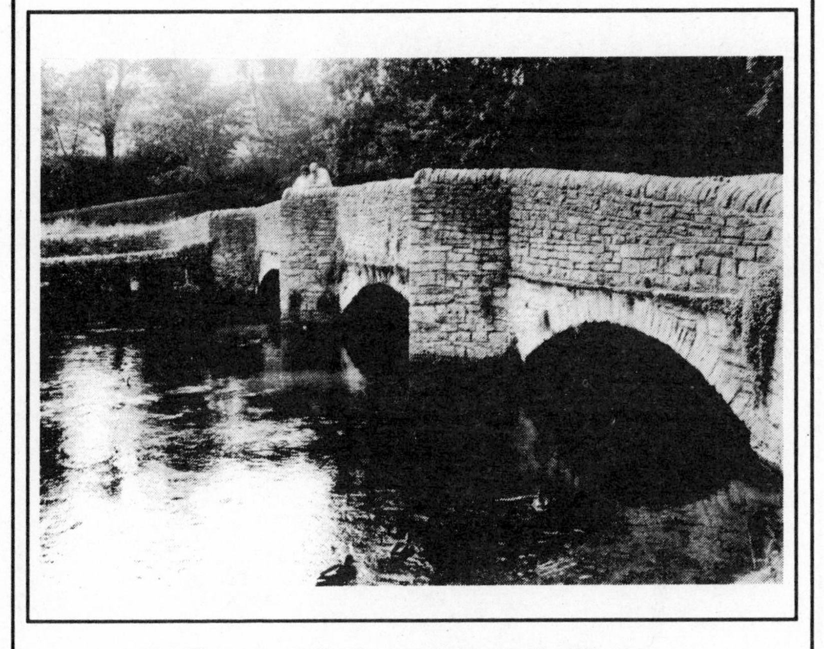

Sheepwash Bridge - Ashford in the Water.

LATHKILL DALE - 11 MILES

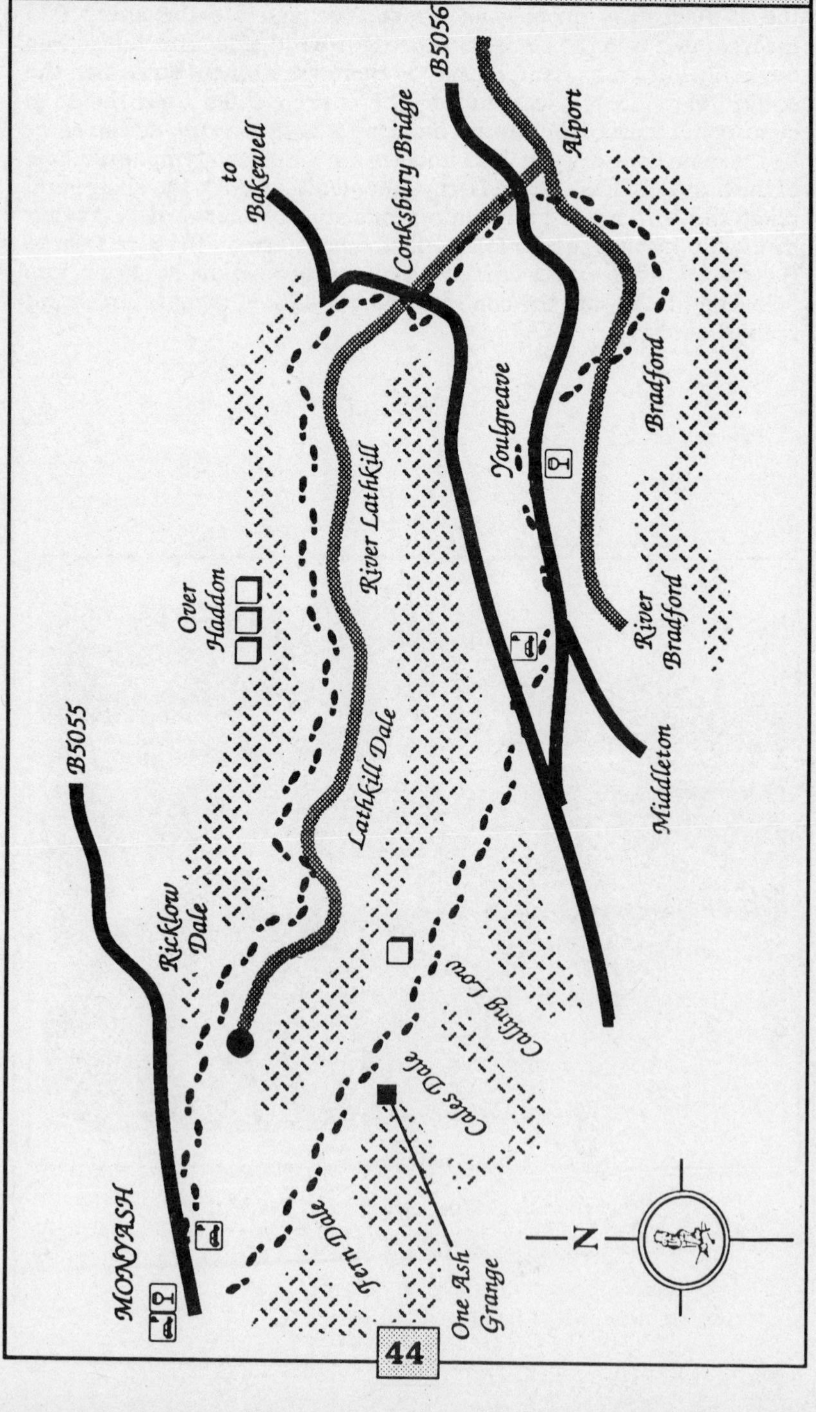

B5056
Alport
Conksbury Bridge
to Bakewell
Youlgreave
Bradford
River Lathkill
Over Haddon
River Bradford
Middleton
B5055
Lathkill Dale
Ricklow Dale
Calling Low
Cales Dale
Fern Dale
One Ash Grange
MONYASH
N

LATHKILL DALE - 11 MILES

- allow 4 hours.

Monyash—Lathkill Dale—Alport—Bradford—Youlgreave—Calling Low—Cales Dale—One Ash Grange—Fern Dale—Monyash.

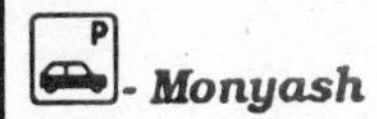

- 1:25,000 Outdoor Leisure Map - The White Peak - East sheet.

- Monyash

Monyash & Youlgreave. Tearoom at farm near Conksbury Bridge.

Terrain: Footpaths through dales and fields. One mile of road walking.

ABOUT THE WALK - Out of all the limestone dales in the Peak District, there is none in my opinion to compare with the qualities of Lathkill Dale. It is steep-sided, wooded and has a clear river and a wealth of flowers and birds. The walk takes you along the whole length of the dale before weaving through Youlgreave village, meadows and historic farms back to Monyash.

WALKING INSTRUCTIONS - Leave Monyash by the Bakewell road and down in the hollow, 1/4 mile from the village, turn right through the stile and enter Lathkill Dale. After two fields you gain the rugged valley with limestone buttresses adorning its sides and soon afterwards cross a slope of boulders which have come from the now disused Ricklow Quarry on your left. This was the source of "Derbyshire Figured" marble, really a Crinoidal limestone and most attractive when polished. The next highlight of this dale is the large cave on your right. During the summer it is dry, but in winter the River Lathkill issues forth the clearest and purest water in England. Not far from the cave on your right is Cales Dale, part of this valley and the right-hand side of Lathkill from here to near Over Haddon being a National Nature Reserve. It was designated on 15th December, 1972, and is the first reserve to be founded in the Peak District National Park. The 158 acres have a remarkable selection of plants, including wood sanicle, herb robert, wood avens, pale wood violet and solomon's seal. Permits are required to visit the reserve.

Shortly after the entrance to Cales Dale, which you cross later, you enter the wooded section of the valley. Part way through this you pass on the right the ruined aqueduct which brought water to Mandale mine where part of the engine house wall is still standing. Emerging from the wood you reach Lathkill Lodge and the road to Over Haddon village on the left. From here to the minor road at Conksbury Bridge is the parkland stretch of Lathkill Dale. Several weirs increase the water flow and the valley is open, reminding one of a city park. The coot and moorhen call and stay on the other side of the river, and the banks are clustered with marsh marigolds.

Turn right at Conksbury Bridge, looking up the valley to see Over Haddon village perched on top of the dale's side. Go past the bridge and 100 yards up the road turn left through the stile and continue through country which is still very open and graceful. At the village of Alport, the end of Lathkill Dale is reached. Cross the minor road, B5056, to the white gate opposite and follow the rough track to the other side as it curves its way to your right beside the river Bradford. On reaching Bradford village, cross the river by the second bridge and take the lefthand road past the houses to Youlgreave church, one of the oldest in the country. The Norman font is the only one of its kind in England, the circular bowl having a holy water stoop included in its design.

From the church, turn left and walk through the village and then take the first road on your right. Climb gradually for 1/4 mile to the second path on your right, after the road to Middleton. Go through the stile and ascend the path to a car park and pic-nic area. Turn left to the road junctions. On your left is the path to Calling Low Farm. Stone stiles guide you and before you reach the farm you walk through the eastern end of Low Moor Plantation. Cross the farmyard and on the other side begin descending through the fields to the edge of Cales Dale. Before you reach the valley look over to your right as this is a good viewpoint down into Lathkill Dale.

At the top of Cales Dale you have a steep but short descent to the valley floor before ascending the opposite side and reaching One Ash Grange, given by the Avenell family in the 12th century to Roche Abbey in South Yorkshire. The abbot would send any misbehaving monks to the Grange as punishment. Continue up the farm track and where this turns sharp right go left through the gate before following close to the right-hand wall in order to reach all the stone stiles. At the top end of

Fern Dale, cross to the other side of the field via a stone stile and continue straight ahead to join the walled track which will bring you back into Monyash. At the road keep straight on so as to reach the cross roads opposite the village green and the market cross which dates back to 1340. This ends the walk and I am sure you will agree with me that Lathkill Dale has no equal.

Lathkill Dale below Over Haddon.

View to OverHaddon from Conksbury Bridge.

THE UPPER DOVE AND MANIFOLD - 12 1/2 MILES

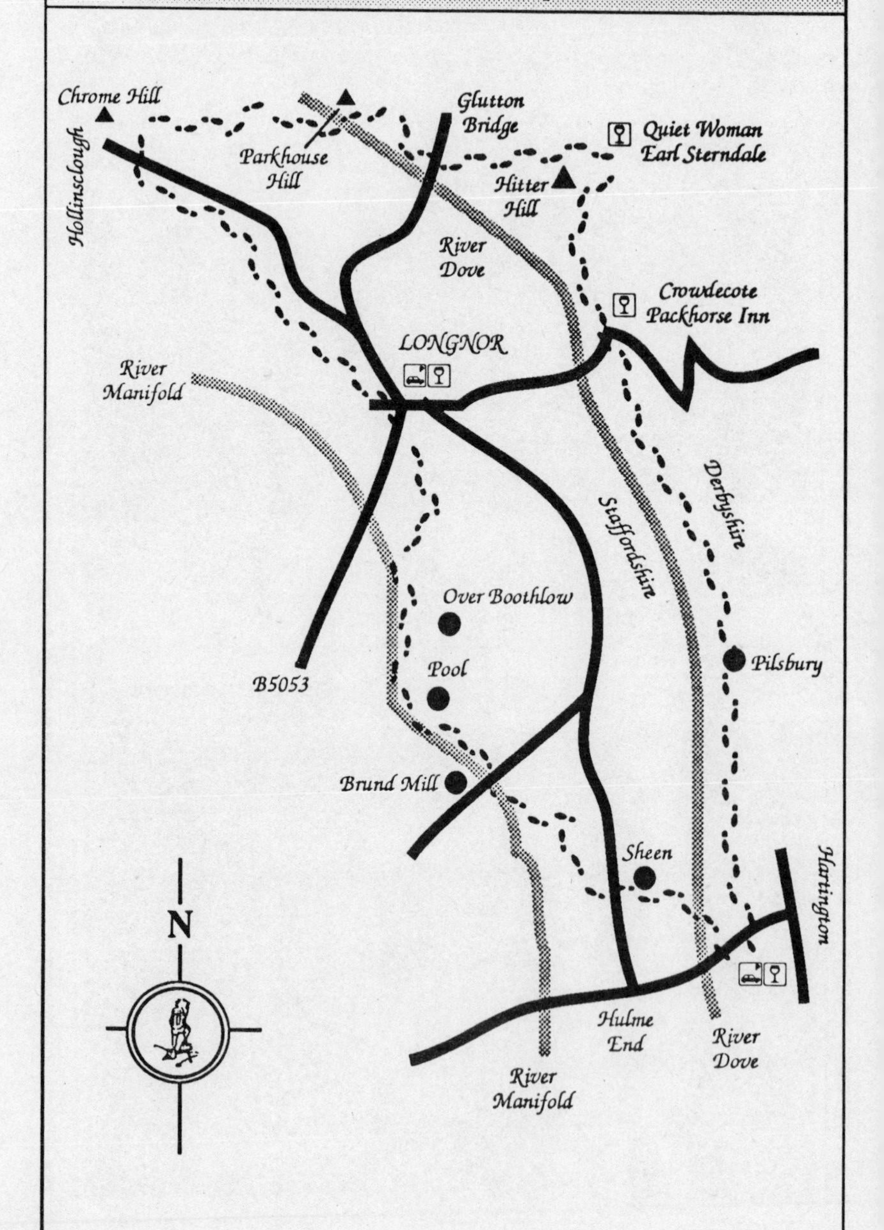

THE UPPER DOVE AND MANIFOLD - 12 1/2 MILES

- allow 4 1/2 hours.

Longnor — Hollinsclough — Parkhouse Hill— Hitter Hill—Earl Sterndale—Crowdecote—Pilsbury —Hartington— Sheen—River Manifold—Longnor.

- 1:25,000 Outdoor Leisure Map - The White Peak - West sheet.

- Longnor Market Place.

- Several in Longnor. Quiet Woman Inn, Earl Sterndale. Packhorse Inn, Crowdecote.

Terrain: Walking through fields and along roads. Gentle ascending and descending.

ABOUT THE WALK - The River's Dove and Manifold provide some of the most scenic and enjoyable walking to be found in the Peak District. The region above Hartington is little known and the paths beside the infant rivers are both quiet and attractive. I have walked this route on a Sunday in the height of summer, and, believe it or not, I did not meet another soul except for cars on the road.

WALKING INSTRUCTIONS - Start from Longnor market place, where high on the central building can be seen a table of tolls, dated 1903, to be charged on market and fair days. Leave the square on its lefthand side and walk through Chapel Street. At the end on the right is Longnor church. rebuilt in 1780 and well worth seeing. The main interest is to find the grave stone to William Billinge who died aged 112 on 30th January 1791.

From the church descend to the minor road, B5053. Turn right and walk along this, and 3/4 mile later take the second road on your left for Hollinsclough. After a short distance along here, the beauty of the region unfolds with the towering hills of Chrome and Parkhouse rising suddenly from the surrounding area. These are reef knolls composed of coral and shell, harder than the surrounding carboniferous limestone which has eroded more rapidly. The lane sides are full of wild flowers—the tall foxglove abounds and large bushes of pink and white roses add richness to the scene.

Approximately half a mile from Hollinsclough the lane curves right and then left. Very soon afterwards on your right is the stile which will lead across the fields to the river Dove under the slopes of Chrome Hill. On reaching the river you have a footbridge and the farm track is on your left—it is most pleasant to sit here and watch dippers, wagtails or warblers. Turn right and follow the track to the minor road beneath the slopes of Parkhouse Hill. Go to the right along the road for a short distance before bearing left, as signposted for Glutton. On reaching the first wall turn right and descend through stiles to the road instead of continuing to Glutton Farm. Cross the road, go through the stile opposite and bear half left to the next stile before curving round Hitter Hill to reach Earl Sterndale.

The main purpose of calling here is to see the pub, The Quiet Woman, where the inn sign shows a woman minus her head. A former owner of the inn went to Longnor market each week and always returned home at the same time. On one occasion he was delayed and his wife sent someone to find out what had happened. This annoyed the owner who on eventually returning home found his wife also annoyed. They had a row about the whole affair and the owner eventually went out and said, *"If I can't have a quiet woman inside, I will have one outside."* He instructed a sign to be painted.

As you entered Earl Sterndale, you would notice another signposted footpath on your right. You now leave the village by this and cross Hitter Hill before descending the hillside to your left to Cave Farm. Here turn left at the track and follow it for about half a mile until it bends sharp left and you can see the stone stile ahead. Go over this and keep straight on, crossing the fields to the minor road just north of Crowdecote. Turn right and walk into the hamlet, and just past the inn go left along the walled farm track which you soon lose as you continue along a path through the meadows close to the river Dove. Leave the Waterside and ascend to the left of Pilsbury Castle, whose earthworks are the remains of a motte and bailey At the other side of the castle join a farm track which brings you to Pilsbury Farm, where keep straight ahead and follow the country lane all the way to Hartington 2 1/4 miles away.

The walk along here is most pleasant and the mere fact that it is a tarmac surface in no way spoils one's enjoyment. It is quiet and peaceful and the only noise is from the farms' animals and machinery. In June and July the scene is one of intense activity as the farmers are busy cutting the hay, rotating it or baling it ready for the barn.

On the right-hand side of the village pond in Hartington is the lane to the factory where the renowned Stilton cheese is made. Just in front of the factory turn right, as signposted, and follow the path across the fields to the footbridge over the river Dove. After this you ascend the valley side, and from the top several stiles guide you to the road to the left of Sheen village. You are now once more back in Staffordshire. Turn right for about one hundred yards until you see the second stone stile on your left. Go over this and cross the fields to the minor road near Moorhouse Farm where turn left and walk to the farm entrance. Again turn left, and almost at the farm building go to the right at the stile alongside the gate. Walk beside the wall past the farm and descend to the minor road just in front of the bridge over the river Manifold and Brund Mill.

Opposite on your right is the stile and footpath which takes you through the Manifold Valley to Pool Farm. Like most of the footpaths on this walk, the stiles are there but the path is rarely trodden This is perfect walking with clumps of ox-eye daisy and ragged robin to be seen. The birds too add enjoyment to the walk—wheatear's hop along the wall in front of you, skylarks singing above, pewit's let out their startled cry and on several occasions I have seen a pair of curlew in this area. On nearing Pool Farm walk past it on your left to reach a stile and then cross the stream via a stone bridge. Soon afterwards you come to a walled lane on the left of the ruined building. Go straight across and follow the faint footpath and clear stiles all the way back to Longnor. About a mile from the lane you walk beside the river Manifold, where all along the banks can be seen large clusters of yellow balsam. On nearing the village turn right through a stone stile and ascend to a farm, entering it from your left. Walk up the farm road to the centre of Longnor, ending a walk you will appreciate for many years.

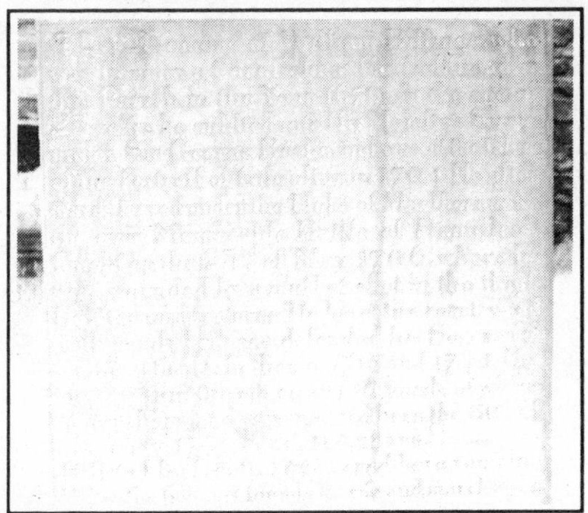

William Billinge tombstone - Longnor churchard.

FOUR DALES - 10 MILES

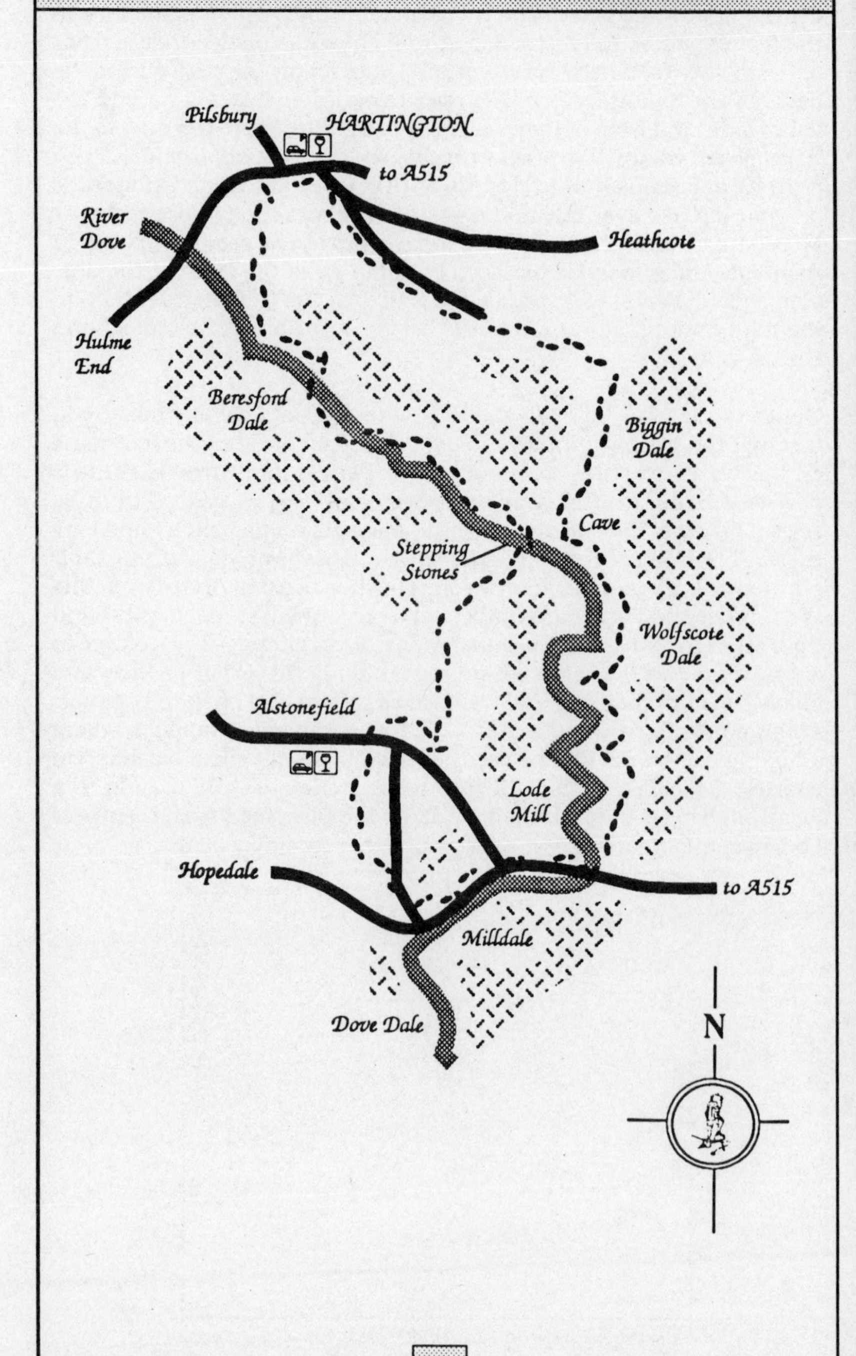

FOUR DALES - 10 MILES

- allow 3 1/2 hours.

Hartington —Biggin Dale— Wolfscote Dale— Milldale—Alstonefield—Wolfscote Dale — Beresford Dale — Hartington.

O.S. MAP ***- 1:25,000 Outdoor Leisure Map - The White Peak - West sheet.***

P ***- The Square, Hartington & Parson's Field, Hartington.***

& tearooms - several in Hartington. Tearoom in Milldale. Inn and tearoom in Alstonefield.

Terrain: Walking along paths through fields and dales.

ABOUT THE WALK - An attractive river, limestone buttresses and graceful trees are features of this walk through some of the Peak District's most attractive scenery. It also has connections with one of the key figures in Peak history, Charles Cotton, while in summer the area is bursting with wild flowers.

WALKING INSTRUCTIONS - From Hartington, nearly opposite the church, take the road on your right beside the war memorial and ascend the hill. Turn up the first road on your right and follow it for a little over one mile, keeping straight ahead at all junctions. Where the road ends there is a footpath down into Biggin Dale turn right in the dale bottom and follow the path through the valley to the river Dove just over one mile away. Biggin Dale is a quiet place, and walking through it is most pleasant. Birds chatter to themselves in the trees and bushes and several blue tits can usually be heard and seen.

At the end of the valley you reach Wolfscote Dale, where turn left and follow the path close to the river. Almost immediately you will see a small cave on your left—it is well worth the short ascent to it, for from the entrance there is one of the best limestone dale views in the area. Wolfscote Dale with its steep buttressed sides lies before you and the river glides along the floor over the weirs, sometimes hidden under the low tree branches. Almost at the base of the cave about fifty yards to the south are the stepping stones across the river. Don't go across but make a mental note of the location for on your return you will use them.

Continue walking down the dale close to the river for just over a mile. Close to the path are a wide range of flowers, predominant being the most attractive and delicate meadow cranesbill which is seen in large clusters. Yellow wild balsam grows along the river banks, and on the limestone buttresses the yellow wall pepper and rock rose sprout in profusion. On reaching the road turn right and cross the bridge before bearing left. On the right-hand side of the bridge is the old Lode Mill—at the rear of the building and partially covered by a corrugated roof is the mill wheel. Follow the road through Milldale village before turning sharp right along the track which eventually passes Alstonefield church. After a short distance along it, turn left as signposted and ascend the fields to reach the track just before the church, a visit to which begins the historical side of the walk.

Much of the present building dates from the 15th century, the main attraction being the oak pews which were carved in 1637/8. On the left of the pulpit can be seen the painted pew of the Cotton family, associated with the river Dove and Beresford Dale where they had their hall which is now destroyed. Charles Cotton, the *"Laureate of the Dove,"* and his faithful companion, Izaak Walton, the renowned fisherman, have used this pew.

Continue past the vicarage and into Alstonefield village, very picturesque with spotless triangular greens and limestone houses having plants growing up their walls. Leave by the Milldale road and just on the outskirts turn left along the rough track as signposted. After about 1/4 mile turn right and follow another rough track which ends at a group of farm buildings. The path from here down to the stepping stones you passed earlier in Wolfscote Dale is little trodden, but all the stone stiles are there and add reassurance. Shortly after leaving the buildings head for the lefthand side of the shallow valley on your right. As you descend, the dale comes into view and below can be seen the river Dove. Using the cave you passed earlier as a guide, you reach the stepping stones.

Once across the river turn left and follow the path beside the Dove all the way back to Hartington. Keep your eyes open for dippers—several inhabit this area and you will see them bobbing up and down on the stones or working their way up the river in search of food. Pass the entrance to Biggin Dale and walk beneath the towering slopes of Wolfscote Dale. Further up the valley you pass a large limestone buttress on your right in which are several caves. A 1/4 mile later you cross the river opposite a road and continue walking up what is now Beresford Dale on its left hand side. Later on you cross the Dove again and leave it as you head over the fields back into Hartington.

At this point you can see ahead on the other side of the river the fishing house used by Cotton and Walton. Over the doorway are two inscribed stones, *"Piscatoribus Sacrum, 1674"* and the initials of Cotton and Walton intertwined—*"I.W."* and *"C.C."* Here they would meet before going fishing, Cotton sitting outside and smoking his pipe which he always referred to as *"his breakfast."*

Wolfscote Dale .

AROUND MATLOCK - 11 MILES

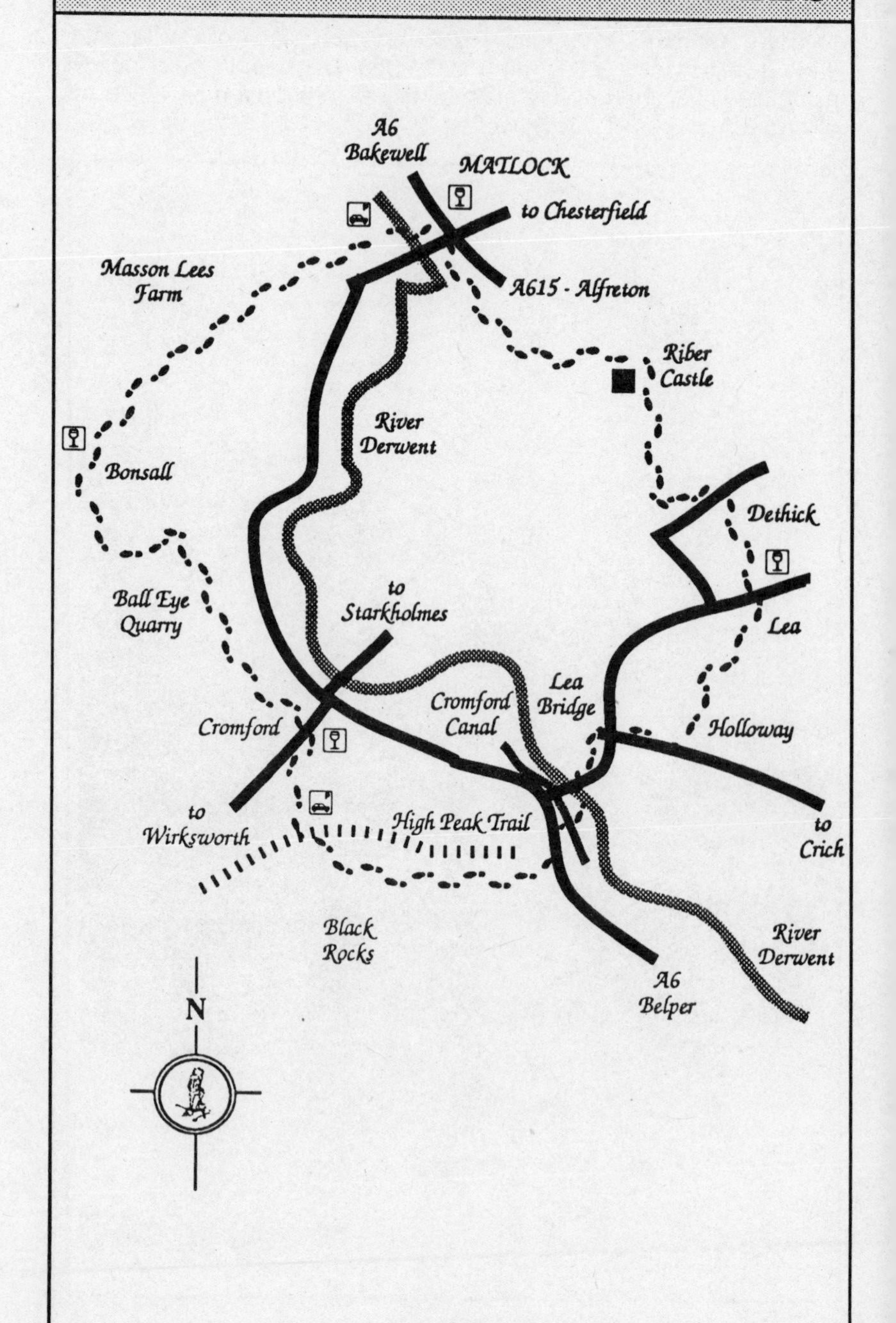

AROUND MATLOCK - 11 MILES

- allow 4 hours.

Matlock — Riber Castle — Dethick — Lea — Holloway — Lea Bridge — High Peak Trail — Cromford — Bonsall — Matlock.

- 1:25,000 Outdoor Leisure Map - The White Peak - East Sheet.

- Central Matlock.

- Several in Matlock. Jug & Glass Inn, Lea. Greyhound Hotel, Cromford. Kings Arms, Bonsall.

Terrain: A hilly walk along footpaths. 2 1/2 miles of road walking linking the walk together.

ABOUT THE WALK - The south-east end of the Peak District National Park and its surrounding area is full of interesting villages, halls and industrial archaeological remains. This walk takes you to several places associated with important figures such as Florence Nightingale and Sir Richard Arkwright as well as the home of the Babington family. The route is rather up and down and roads are used to join it together, but don't let this put you off for it is a grand walk with distant views and much to see.

WALKING INSTRUCTIONS - From the main roundabout in Matlock, close to the bridge over the river Derwent, walk through the pleasure gardens. Towards the end cross a small bridge and continue straight ahead. On meeting the "No Through Road" known as Stoney Way, turn right and ascend this to Church Street where a signpost points to your right and indicates that the footpath to Riber is 1/4 mile along the road. On the way visit the Matlock parish church of St. Giles which contains several interesting items. The octagonal font is over 700 years old, and was replaced in the church in 1924 after lying in the rectory garden for many years. On the left hand side of the door is a small recess, where in a glass case are six "crantses." These funeral garlands are some of the best preserved examples to be seen today. The stained glass windows are particularly beautiful, especially the east window above the altar which was made in 1969.

On the right-hand side of the entrance to Highfields School is the footpath signpost and path to Riber. Now your work begins—although it is a short ascent; it is also steep. A magnificent view unfolds the higher you get, and you have many an excuse to stop and regain your breath before continuing! The whole of Matlock and Darley Dale lies before you with Stanton Moor and the Earl Grey tower or your left. Looming infront all the time is the stark shell of Riber Castle, built by John Smedley, a local hosiery manufacturer, in 1868. The building was later used as a boys' school until 1929, and during the war became a food store. In 1962 a group of zoologists. purchased the shell for £540.

At the castle turn left and descend into Riber village. At the "T" junction on your right can be seen the signpost and footpath for Tansley. Follow this and, after the first field, cross a rough track. On entering a third field turn sharp right towards a stone stile ahead of you. In the summer the fields are full of tall grass with buttercups and ox-eye daisies growing in profusion. Keep to the faint path and cross a minor road—the stone stiles act as guides to your route. In due course you reach and turn left onto the road in front of Littlemoor Wood. A 1/4 mile later turn left, as signposted, and after half a mile of road walking reach Dethick hamlet on your right.

I know of no other place in Derbyshire which matches the peaceful setting of Dethick. The road to it, the neat little cluster of buildings and the church tower all complete the picture. Part way through the hamlet turn right down the walled lane to the church, where a frieze contains the now weather-worn shields of the Babington and other local families. Anthony Babington was the key figure in the ill-fated plot to release Mary, Queen of Scots from Wingfield Manor. The plot was discovered and he was executed at Lincoln's Inn Fields in September 1586.

Leave the church by the metal kissing gate on your left and follow the footpath down across the field close to a wood on your right. A little further on go to the right and descend through the trees, cross a stream and climb to the road in Lea village. Turn right and then left opposite the Jug and Glass Inn, ascend briefly and at the "Y" junction by the post office turn right. At the end of the lane, where it curves to your left, keep straight ahead. On your right is a footpath which crosses a minor road before descending through the trees to Holloway. In the village turn left and walk along the road—over on your right you have distant views of your walk with- the Black Rocks of Cromford standing out prominently. At the road junction in front of the Florence Nightingale Memorial Hall turn right and descend to Lea Bridge.

Over on your left, although hidden by trees in summer is Lea Hurst. Here the renowned Lady of the Lamp Florence Nightingale, spent part of her life. The hall remained in the Nightingale family until Louis S. Nightingale died in 1940, and is now used as a home for the elderly At the bottom of the hill you pass the works of John Smedley, who built Riber Castle last century. Continue along the road, and on your left on the right-hand bend is a footpath. Follow this across the footbridge over the river Derwent, and past the sewerage works to the Cromford Canal and the High Peak Trail.

The Cromford Canal was built by Arkwright in 1793. Here in June moorhens with their young can be seen in the reeds. On the other side of the canal is the High Peak railway, built in 1830 by Josiah Jessop and connecting with the Peak Forest Canal at Whaley Bridge. Because of the nature of the terrain, in several places the train was winched up by a stationary engine, and the section you walk up is one of these inclines. Many of the railway accessories can still be seen as you go up the cinder path to the Black Rocks This trail is similar to the Tissington Trail and was officially opened to the public in 1972.

After reaching the summit of the incline, with the engine building on your left, you realise the ascent was worth it for over to your right you have one of the best views of Derbyshire. Below is Cromford where the mills of Arkwright can be spotted along with his home, Willersley Castle, in which he never lived. Beyond, the red tower of Masson Mill sticks its head above the trees. The houses of Matlock Bank hug the valley side, and crowning the skyline on your right is the sombre ruin of Riber Castle.

Underneath the high buttresses of the Black Rocks of Cromford is the car park. Here you turn right, as signposted, and descend towards the village of Cromford, emerging on to the road where you turn right and descend the hill. Sir Richard Arkwright, the cotton spinning genius, brought the first water-powered spinning mill in the world
to Cromford in 1771. Through his drive and energy the factory system as we know it today was born, and by the time he died in 1792 he had personally amassed a fortune of £500,000. Much of Cromford was built by him and little has altered since his day.

In front of the Greyhound Hotel turn left and walk past a mill pond on your right. On the village outskirts you will see a group of houses, also on your right, with an ascending flagged path in front. Climb this through the trees—the route finding may be awkward as the quarry has gobbled up the original line of the path. However, a good quarry track exists and by using this you will reach Bonsall. The church to St. James, which you pass on your left, is worth a visit if time permits. The tower is attractive and inside are many beautiful arrays of stained-glass windows. Continue down the road to the market cross—a magnificent example with thirteen steps. Here in the olden days people would sit with their butter and eggs and sell them to passers-by.

From the cross walk up the road and take the concrete path on your right. Follow it for about 1/4 mile before leaving it by going through a stile on your right, crossing the fields and descending to the left-hand side of Masson Lees Farm. The path here is not clear but the stiles are all there, so you should have no difficulty. As you descend you have a marvellous view of Matlock and Riber in front of you. At the farm, cross the track and continue down the path which becomes clearer. You arrive in the centre of Matlock close to the bridge over the River Derwent, where the walk ends.

Black Rocks of Cromford.

THE HIKER'S CODE

- *Hike only along marked routes - do not leave the trail.*
- *Use stiles to climb fences; close gates.*
- *Camp only in designated campsites.*
- *Carry a light-weight stove.*
- *Leave the trail cleaner than you found it.*
- *Leave flowers and plants for others to enjoy.*
- *Keep dogs on a leash.*
- *Protect and do not disturb wildlife.*
- *Use the trail at your own risk.*
- *Leave only your thanks and footprints - take nothing but photographs.*

THE RIVER DOVE - 9 MILES

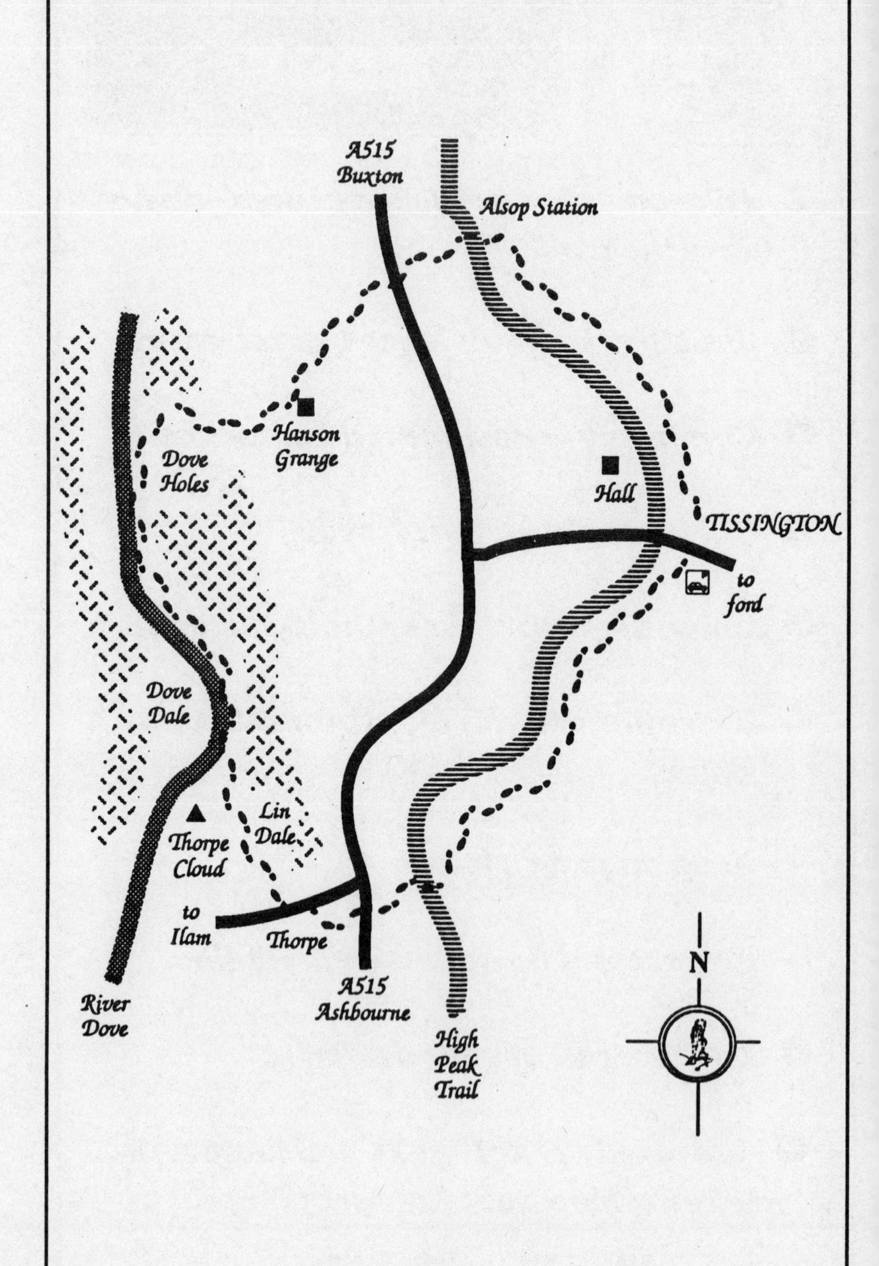

THE RIVER DOVE - 9 MILES

- allow 3 1/2 hours.

Tissington Station—Tissington Trail—Thorpe— Lin Dale—Dovedale—Hanson Grange—Alsop-en -le-Dale Station—Tissington.

- 1:25,000 Outdoor Leisure Map - The White Peak - East & West sheets.

- Tissington Station.

- Dog & Partridge, Thorpe. Tearoom at Tissington.

Terrain: Trail walking, footpaths across fields and in dales.

ABOUT THE WALK - This route combines two aspects of the limestone countryside which make walking in it a constant pleasure — the Tissington Trail and Dovedale. The beauty of Dove dale is well known and has attracted the visitor for centuries, but the Tissington Trail is new and brings an added dimension to walking in the Peak District.

WALKING INSTRUCTIONS - From Tissington station walk southwards for about 1 1/2 miles along the trail, a disused railway line which was opened by the London and North Western company in 1899 and ran from Buxton to Ashbourne. The line was completely closed to traffic in 1967, and in the following year was purchased by the Peak Park Planning Board which began the work of converting it into a walkable trail. All the old railway stations were removed and many of the buildings and surrounding areas converted into car parks and picnic sites. The track was lifted and the limestone ballast covered with tons of soil before seeding. On 5th June, 1971, the trail was officially opened to the public.

Pass Thorpe Station and 1/4 mile later, turn right as signposted and cross the fields to the outskirts of Thorpe. At the minor road go straight across and descend along the lane into the village, proceeding towards

Ilam, at the cross-roads. Opposite the first road on your left, turn right as signposted at the public topilets and small car park. Go through the fields, descending along the footpath under the slopes of Thorpe Cloud and through Lin Dale. In a little over half a mile you reach Dove Dale where flows the river Dove, one of the fisherman's favourite waters. Turn right and follow the wide path through the entire length of the valley.

Dove Dale is a masterpiece of nature whose rock pin nacles, woodland and river combine to make a captivating picture. As you walk up the dale you pass many interesting features. Shortly after joining the path you see on the lefthand side twelve limestone pinnacles known as the Twelve Apostles, the nearest one being St. Peter. Next you ascend to a height known as Lover's Leap. The legend behind this is that a young lady was jilted by her boy friend, so she decided to end her life. She climbed to this point and jumped hoping to kill herself against the rocks at the bottom, but the numerous bushes cushioned her fall and she was able to get up and walk away! From that day she forgot her broken love affair and is reputed to have lived happily ever after.

More pinnacles known as the Tissington Spires precede the impressive Reynards Cave, reached by a steep and rocky climb through the archway on your right. After the cave the dale narrows and the path is pushed to the river's edge at a point known as "The Straights." Lion Rock, which bulges over the path, portrays the face of a lion. Hidden during the summer by the trees above is a large square boulder known as the Watch Tower. After this the dale opens out slightly and you have the limestone pinnacles of Pickering's Tor on your right, while on the opposite side of the river is Ilam Rock. About one hundred feet high, it was first climbed in 1850 and today, because of the looseness of the rock, is an alarming ascent. Just round the corner you come to Dove Holes, two shallow limestone caves of which the largest has an entrance seventy feet high.

Just after Dove Holes turn right and ascend the shallow dale to Hanson Grange Farm. At the other side of this join the farm track and follow it to the minor road. Cross over and follow the path to the A515 and Alsop-en le-Dale station opposite. Turn right and follow the Tissington trail back to Tissington, three miles away. The bank sides are full of wild flowers, including cowslips, red campion, germander speedwell, yellow archangel, bluebells, forget-me-nots and common vetch. In due course you reach your starting point, and if you have time available a look at Tissington village, its hall and church is a decided climax to the walk.

The Tissington Trail near Thorpe.

Tissington Hall.

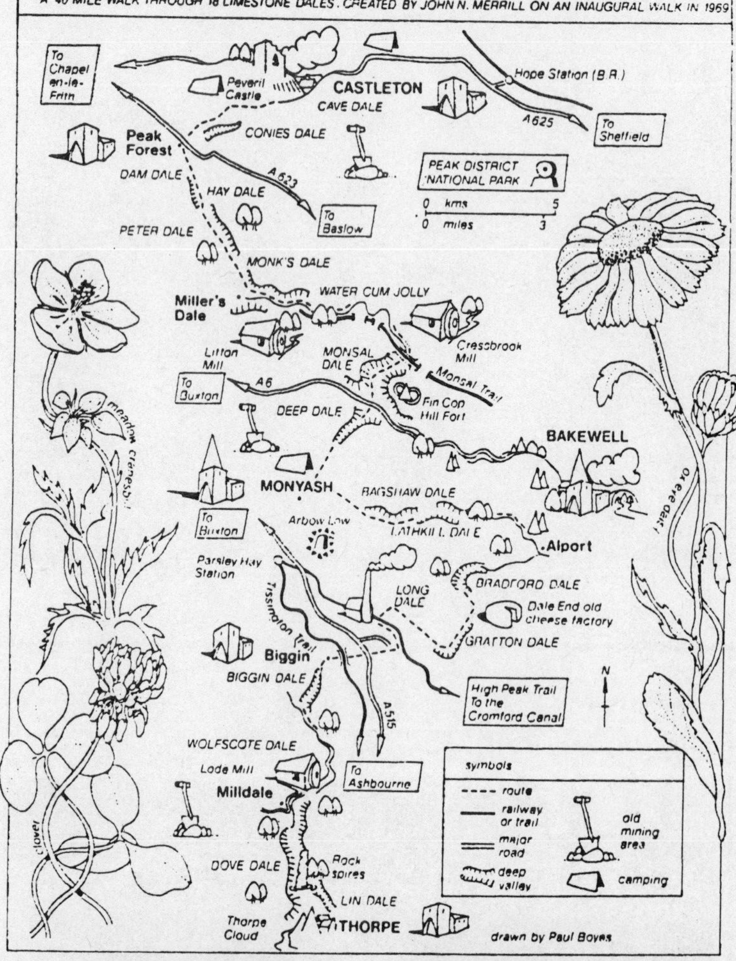

John Merrill Peakland Way (100 miles) walkers at Ashbourne.

THREE LONG DISTANCE WALKS

For the person wanting a longer route or one which presents a challenge, the following three walks rank as my favourites, Only the key points of the route are given. These three walks combine all the characteristics to be found in Peakland walking.

The Gritstone Edge Walk - 15 1/2 miles.

Makes an ideal Christmas or New Year's Day walk. Basically the route is: Moscar Lodge—Stanage Edge— Cowper Stone—Burbage Edge—Longshaw Estate—Froggatt Edge—Curbar Edge—Baslow Edge—Baslow.
Can be extended to start from Derwent Reservoir - see John Merrill's *"Peak District End to End Walks"* book.

The Derwent Watershed Walk - 40 miles.

The toughest walk in the Peak District. Should only be attempted by experienced parties. It can be done in two halves using the Snake road as the break, but it is more of a challenge to do it all in one day. About twelve hours is needed. The route: Yorkshire Bridge (Bamford) — Win Hill—Lose Hill—Mam Tor—Rushup Edge—Brown Knoll — Kinder Downfall — Mill Hill —Moss Castle —Snake Road—Bleaklow Stones—Swains Head—How den Edge—Rocking Stones—Margery Hill—Featherbed Moss—Back Tor—Dovestone Tor—White Tor—Moscar—High Neb—Yorkshire Bridge.
See John Merrill's book - *"Circular Walks on Kinder & Bleaklow."*

The Limey Way - 40 miles

A walk right through the limestone dales from Castleton to the end of Dovedale. This route was inaugurated by myself in June 1969. This likewise can be done in two sections using Monyash as the half way point, but again it is more of a challenge to do it all at once. About twelve hours is needed. The route: Castleton—Cave Dale—Old Moor—Peak Forest—Dam Dale—Hay Dale—Wheston — Monksdale House— Millers Dale —Cressbrook Mill—Monsal Dale—Deep Dale—Monyash—Lathkill Dale—Bradford Dale—Smerrill Grange—Gratton Dale —Long Dale—Friden—Biggin—Biggin Dale—Wolfscote Dale—Milldale—Dovedale—Stepping Stones - Lin Dale - Thorpe.
See John Merrill's book - *"The Limey Way."*

WALK RECORD CHART

Date walked -

GRITSTONE WALKS -

ALPORT CASTLES - 12 MILES ....

KINDER DOWNFALL - 8 MILES ....

DERWENT EDGE - 9 MILES ....

THE PEAKLAND RIDGE -9 MILES ....

MOOR AND VILLAGE -12 MILES ....

EDGE AND RIVER - 9 MILES ....

CHATSWORTH PARK - 9 MILES ....

LIMESTONE WALKS -

THE RIVER WYE - 9 MILES..

MONSAL DALE - 9 MILES ....

LATHKILL DALE - 11 MILES ....

THE UPPER DOVE

AND MANIFOLD - 12 1/2 MILES ....

FOUR DALES - 10 MILES ....

AROUND MATLOCK - 11 MILES ....

THE RIVER DOVE - 9 MILES ....

THREE LONG WALKS ....

....

....

THE JOHN MERRILL WALK BADGE

Complete six of the walks in this book and get the above special John Merrill badge and signed certificate. Badges are black cloth with lettering and walking man embroidered in four colours and measure 3 1/2" diamater.

BADGE ORDER FORM

Date and details of walks completed..

....

NAME ....

ADDRESS ....

....

Price: £3.00 each including postage, VAT and signed completion certificate.
Amount enclosed (Payable to El Morro Equipment Ltd) ..

From: El Morro Equipment Ltd.,
Milne House, Speedwell Mill, Millers Green,
Wirksworth,, Derbyshire. DE4 4BL.
✆ /Fax (0629) 826354 - 24hr answering service.

********** *YOU MAY PHOTOCOPY THIS FORM* ***********

"I'VE DONE A JOHN MERRILL WALK" T SHIRT -

Emerald Green with white lettering and walking man logo. Send £7.50 to El Morro Equipment Ltd., stating size required.

John Merrill's "Happy Walking!" Cap - £3.00

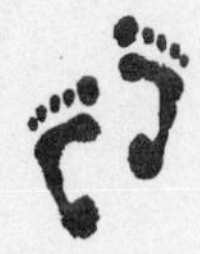

"from footprint to finished book"

OTHER BOOKS by John N. Merrill Published by TRAIL CREST PUBLICATIONS Ltd.

CIRCULAR WALK GUIDES -

SHORT CIRCULAR WALKS IN THE PEAK DISTRICT - Vol. 1 and 2
CIRCULAR WALKS IN WESTERN PEAKLAND
SHORT CIRCULAR WALKS IN THE STAFFORDSHIRE MOORLANDS
SHORT CIRCULAR WALKS - TOWNS & VILLAGES OF THE PEAK DISTRICT
SHORT CIRCULAR WALKS AROUND MATLOCK
SHORT CIRCULAR WALKS IN THE DUKERIES
SHORT CIRCULAR WALKS IN SOUTH YORKSHIRE
SHORT CIRCULAR WALKS IN SOUTH DERBYSHIRE
SHORT CIRCULAR WALKS AROUND BUXTON
SHORT CIRCULAR WALKS AROUND WIRKSWORTH
SHORT CIRCULAR WALKS IN THE HOPE VALLEY
40 SHORT CIRCULAR WALKS IN THE PEAK DISTRICT
CIRCULAR WALKS ON KINDER & BLEAKLOW
SHORT CIRCULAR WALKS IN SOUTH NOTTINGHAMSHIRE
SHIRT CIRCULAR WALKS IN CHESHIRE
SHORT CIRCULAR WALKS IN WEST YORKSHIRE
CIRCULAR WALKS TO PEAK DISTRICT AIRCRAFT WRECKS by John Mason
CIRCULAR WALKS IN THE DERBYSHIRE DALES
SHORT CIRCULAR WALKS IN EAST DEVON
SHORT CIRCULAR WALKS AROUND HARROGATE
SHORT CIRCULAR WALKS IN CHARNWOOD FOREST
SHORT CIRCULAR WALKS AROUND CHESTERFIELD
SHORT CIRCULAR WALKS IN THE YORKS DALES - Vol 1 - Southern area.
SHORT CIRCULAR WALKS IN THE AMBER VALLEY (Derbyshire)
SHORT CIRCULAR WALKS IN THE LAKE DISTRICT
SHORT CIRCULAR WALKS IN THE NORTH YORKSHIRE MOORS
SHORT CIRCULAR WALKS IN EAST STAFFORDSHIRE
DRIVING TO WALK - 16 Short Circular walks south of London by Dr. Simon Archer
LONG CIRCULAR WALKS IN THE PEAK DISTRICT - Vol.1 and 2.
LONG CIRCULAR WALKS IN THE STAFFORDSHIRE MOORLANDS
LONG CIRCULAR WALKS IN CHESHIRE
WALKING THE TISSINGTON TRAIL
WALKING THE HIGH PEAK TRAIL
WALKING THE MONSAL TRAIL & OTHER DERBYSHIRE TRAILS

CANAL WALKS -

VOL 1 - DERBYSHIRE & NOTTINGHAMSHIRE
VOL 2 - CHESHIRE & STAFFORDSHIRE
VOL 3 - STAFFORDSHIRE
VOL 4 - THE CHESHIRE RING
VOL 5 - LINCOLNSHIRE & NOTTINGHAMSHIRE
VOL 6 - SOUTH YORKSHIRE
VOL 7 - THE TRENT & MERSEY CANAL

JOHN MERRILL DAY CHALLENGE WALKS -

WHITE PEAK CHALLENGE WALK
DARK PEAK CHALLENGE WALK
PEAK DISTRICT END TO END WALKS
STAFFORDSHIRE MOORLANDS CHALLENGE WALK
THE LITTLE JOHN CHALLENGE WALK

YORKSHIRE DALES CHALLENGE WALK
NORTH YORKSHIRE MOORS CHALLENGE WALK
LAKELAND CHALLENGE WALK
THE RUTLAND WATER CHALLENGE WALK
MALVERN HILLS CHALLENGE WALK
THE SALTER'S WAY
THE SNOWDON CHALLENGE
CHARNWOOD FOREST CHALLENGE WALK
THREE COUNTIES CHALLENGE WALK (Peak District).
CAL-DER-WENT WALK by Geoffrey Carr,
THE QUANTOCK WAY

INSTRUCTION & RECORD -
HIKE TO BE FIT.....STROLLING WITH JOHN
THE JOHN MERRILL WALK RECORD BOOK

MULTIPLE DAY WALKS -
THE RIVERS'S WAY
PEAK DISTRICT: HIGH LEVEL ROUTE
PEAK DISTRICT MARATHONS
THE LIMEY WAY
THE PEAKLAND WAY

COAST WALKS & NATIONAL TRAILS -
ISLE OF WIGHT COAST PATH
PEMBROKESHIRE COAST PATH
THE CLEVELAND WAY
WALKING ANGELSEY'S COASTLINE.

CYCLING *Compiled by Arnold Robinson.*
CYCLING AROUND THE NORTH YORK MOORS
CYCLING AROUND CASTLETON & the Hope Valley.

PEAK DISTRICT HISTORICAL GUIDES -
A to Z GUIDE OF THE PEAK DISTRICT
DERBYSHIRE INNS - an A to Z guide
HALLS AND CASTLES OF THE PEAK DISTRICT & DERBYSHIRE
TOURING THE PEAK DISTRICT & DERBYSHIRE BY CAR
DERBYSHIRE FOLKLORE
PUNISHMENT IN DERBYSHIRE
CUSTOMS OF THE PEAK DISTRICT & DERBYSHIRE
WINSTER - a souvenir guide
ARKWRIGHT OF CROMFORD
LEGENDS OF DERBYSHIRE
DERBYSHIRE FACTS & RECORDS
TALES FROM THE MINES by Geoffrey Carr
PEAK DISTRICT PLACE NAMES by Martin Spray

JOHN MERRILL'S MAJOR WALKS -
TURN RIGHT AT LAND'S END
WITH MUSTARD ON MY BACK
TURN RIGHT AT DEATH VALLEY
EMERALD COAST WALK

SKETCH BOOKS -
SKETCHES OF THE PEAK DISTRICT

COLOUR BOOK:-
THE PEAK DISTRICT.......something to remember her by.

OVERSEAS GUIDES -
HIKING IN NEW MEXICO - Vol I - The Sandia and Manzano Mountains.
Vol 2 - Hiking "Billy the Kid" Country. Vol 4 - N.W. area - " Hiking Indian Country."
"WALKING IN DRACULA COUNTRY" - Romania.

VISITOR'S GUIDES -
MATLOCK. BAKEWELL. ASHBOURNE.

EQUIPMENT NOTES
.... some personal thoughts

BOOTS - *preferably with a full leather upper, of medium weight, with a vibram sole. I always add a foam cushioned insole to help cushion the base of my feet.*

SOCKS - *I generally wear two thick pairs as this helps minimise blisters. The inner pair are of loop stitch variety and approximately 80% wool. The outer are a thick rib pair of approximately 80% wool.*

WATERPROOFS - *for general walking I wear a T shirt or cotton shirt with a cotton wind jacket on top. You generate heat as you walk and I prefer to layer my clothes to avoid getting too hot. Depending on the seasonwill dictate how many layers you wear. In soft rain I just use my wind jacket for I know it quickly dries out. In heavy or consistant rain I slip on a neoprene lined cagoule, and although hot and clammy it does keep me reasonably dry. Only in extreme conditions will I don overtrousers, much preferring to get wet and feel comfortable. I never wear gaiters!*

FOOD - *as I walk I carry bars of chocolate, for they provide instant energy and are light to carry. In winter a flask of hot coffee is welcome. I never carry water and find no hardship from not doing so, but this is a personal matter! From experience I find the more I drink the more I want and sweat. You should always carry some extra food such as Kendal Mint Cake, for emergencies.*

RUCKSACKS - *for day walking I use a climbing rucksack of about 40 litre capacity and although it leaves excess space it does mean that the sac is well padded, with an internal frame and padded shoulder straps. Inside apart from the basics for one day I carry gloves, balaclava, spare pullover and a pair of socks.*

MAP & COMPASS - *when I am walking I always have the relevant map - preferably 1:25,000 scale - open in my hand. This enables me to constantly check that I am walking the right way. In case of bad weather I carry a compass, which once mastered gives you complete confidence in thick cloud or mist.*